GOD'S CALL UPON YOUR LIFE

Stretch Your Spiritual Muscles, Into Your Call

Rose A. Juma

authorHOUSE®

AuthorHouse™
1663 Liberty Drive, Suite 200
Bloomington, IN 47403
www.authorhouse.com
Phone: 1-800-839-8640

First published by AuthorHouse 3/16/2009

ISBN: 978-1-4389-5256-7 (sc)

Printed in the United States of America
Bloomington, Indiana

This book is printed on acid-free paper.

Acknowledgement

First, I would like to thank the Almighty God, through His son Jesus Christ, our LORD and saviour; for giving me this revelation, strength and courage to bring to His people what He wanted them to know and have.

This works is totally inspired by the Holy Spirit, and I take no credit for it. All the scriptures have been taken from the Holy Bible: authorized King James Version with translation out of the original tongues.

I am grateful for all those who have been my pastors and teachers and help guide me in my Christian walk. These include Pastor Bea Coleman, Pastor Carol and Charles Furman of Miracle Healing Faith Center, Schweinfurt, Germany. Also my present pastors Stan and Gerry Moore of Words of Life, Miami Florida.

I thank those who have always encouraged, challenged and supported me including Ms. Donna Hilley, Bestman Dokubo and much thanks to my son Desmond and daughter Hildah whose love I cherish.

To God be the Glory.

Forward

Everything depends on God. That's why we have success in everything we do. In him you find a friend, an advocate of leadership and comforter in all situations. I agreed to write the foreword for this book because it is part of Gods work and I always wanted to be part of Gods work.

Rose has been preaching to me for more than a decade, she has led many individuals to a relationship with God including me. Rose is a winner in everything she does and that begun when she decided to walk with God since she was a little girl, I am always fascinated by her teachings and also she uses her life experience as an example of how one can conquer difficult circumstances.

Rose has success and is blessed with a pastoring potential that has reached and changed many lost souls. My opinion is simple: read this book "Gods call upon your life". If you do, your spiritual muscles will be stretched and your faith level will definitely increase, plus your life will be transformed forever.

Desmond Barack Okoth

Dedication

This Book is dedicated to the Holy Spirit of the Living God who gave the revelation, inspiration, direction and the guidance to write it.

Contents

CHAPTER ONE

Your Heart's desire

Have you been asking God to use you? Is it your heart's desire for God to use you? Then this is your booklet. This is meant to be a guide for those who are seeking to be used by God as vessels, to bring God's Kingdom upon the earth. Those, who have not yet pined down exactly what God has called them to do, Those, who still have questions and are desperately looking for answers.

Have you been moving from church to church and still feel that you haven't reached home yet? Have you been moving from one Ministry to another and still can't seem to settle down?

Are you tired of sitting in the pew all these years? Do you feel like being up there and singing in the choir or being an usher or the bookstore manager of your church and yet you are not quiet sure whether that is what God has called you to do?

Do you feel so sure that you are gifted in singing, evangelization, preaching, teaching, prophecy, etc. and yet it seems like you are not being given that chance in your church?

Have you been crying and saying "God use me, Let me be your vessel and use me as you will. I am ready, sent me Oh Lord and I will go wherever you want me to go, and I will do whatever you want me to do?

Have you been crying to God to show you the plan and purpose for your life; for Him to bring to pass, the reason why He created you?

The Holy Spirit is our helper and He will help you accomplish this desire.

If you answered YES to any of these questions, or any other that I didn't mention but is in this category, and you want answers NOW. Then this is a guide for you.

The word of God says;

"Delight thyself also in the Lord: trust also in Him;
and He shall give you the desires of thine heart."
(Psalms 37: 4)

Many books have been written guiding people on how to become rich, wealthy, how to become millionaires and how to think and grow rich. The authors actually are ready to take you by the hand and guide you in becoming a millionaire.

Well this handbook will do, just that for you. It will guide you on how to walk in the call of God upon your life.

One thing I want to make clear here before I say much, is that, God's grace and mercy is unearnable. No matter what we do, we can not earn God's grace and mercy. It is freely given. What this book is doing is to help you position yourself to receive whatever God has prepared for you. So that it comes forth and manifest. For by grace are ye saved through faith; and that not of yourselves: it is a gift of God: Not of works, lest any man should boast. (Ephesians 2: 8-9). For it is not by might nor by power but by the Spirit, saith the LORD. So, when you start seeing the manifestation of God's call upon your life, it is not because of what you have done. It is a gift of God. All you've done, is positioned yourself in the right place to receive what the Giver, God has for you.

Now, WARNING!! This is a life style, not a one time thing. It is diligence, painstaking and patience. Like a good soldier is always meant to be ready to serve at all times.

You will have to stretch your spiritual muscles, and keep on, no matter how hard it feels. This book will show you how to be in the presence of God 24/7. Like Paul, you will have to <u>press toward the mark.</u>

" I press toward the mark, for the prize of the high calling of God in Christ
Jesus." (Philippians 3: 14)

Don't be like the multitude that simply pressed, but go a step further and touch with a purpose - to receive,

" And Jesus said who touched me? When all denied, Peter and they that
were with him said, <u>Master, the multitude throng thee and press</u> thee, and
sayest thou who touched me?"(Luke 8 :45)

Rather be like the woman with the issue of blood. She must have thought to herself, if I could only touch the border (or the hem) of His garment. Then she acted upon her thought, her faith, and her pressing was different, she went a step further and touched. She pressed toward a goal that she had set in her heart, in her mind.

Her faith, her action and her determination, required her to even bend. Bending is not comfortable, especially, amidst a great multitude, thronging. So she not only pressed but also bended to touch the hem of Jesus garment. All these package, magnetized the healing virtue from the Lord Jesus to flow through to her.

This guide will show you to press toward, to bend, to touch, and eventually, your faith and action will magnetize the call of God upon your life to manifest itself in a mighty way. You will be humbled by the faithfulness of our Almighty God, when this happens. I have felt this many times in my life. And you will too.

Bible Personalities:

Let us start by looking at the pattern of God's call upon those He used as vessels. We will look at a few individuals.

Most of those that God used, were called before they were born. So, as they came into the world, they already had a predestined call of God upon their lives. This we see in the birth of Samson (Judges 13:1-25), John the Baptist (Luke 1:5-17), and even our Lord Jesus Christ that was prophesied by the prophets.

"Now all this was done, that it might be fulfilled which was spoken of the Lord by the prophet, saying, behold, a virgin shall bring forth a son, and they shall call his name Emmanuel, which being interpreted is, God with us."
(Mathew 1: 22-23)

We see this in Jeremiah's call too. The word of the Lord came unto Jeremiah saying:

"Before I formed thee in the belly I knew thee; and before thou camest forth out of the womb I sanctified thee, and ordained thee a prophet unto the nations."
(Jeremiah 1: 4-5)

Paul, while writing to the Romans, touches on this issue, he says in his letter:

"And we know that all things work together for good to them that love God, to them who are the called according to His purpose. For whom He did foreknow, He also did predestinate to be conformed to the image of his Son, that He might be the firstborn among many brethren. Moreover whom He did predestinate, them he also called; and whom He called, them He also justified and whom He justified, them He also glorified."(Romans 8: 28-30)

That should make you shout hallelujah, because it confirms what you already know. That God foreknew you, predestinated you, called you, justified you and also glorified you, no matter what might be going on in your life right now.

This, however, was not always the case with all those God used in the Bible. This would be limiting our God and making other people feel left out. Actually, some people who do not search the scriptures, have sometimes used the first part of Revelation 7: 3-8 to end up not seeing their share in the second coming of our LORD Jesus. They have felt left out because of the 144,000 of all tribes of Israel being given the seal of our God on their foreheads.

What they have done is not to read the rest of the chapter Revelation 7 : 9-17 to see that all are actually included therein, in the "multitude." I thank God for his grace and mercy. As long as you have believed in your heart and confessed with your mouth that Jesus Christ is the son of God and that He came and died and on the third day He rose again, and is seated at the right hand of the Father. Then you are in the multitude that John beheld.

" After this I beheld and lo, a great multitude which no man could number, of all nations, and kindreds, and people, and tongues, stood before the throne, and before the Lamb, clothed with white robes, and palms in their hands" (Revelation 7: 9)

Going back to our point, we see that some of those that God used, as vessels, to do mighty things, were actually called by God because He saw their hearts.

"But the LORD said unto Samuel, Look not on his countenance, or on the height of his stature; because I have refused him: for the LORD seeth not as man seeth; for man looketh on the outward appearance, but the LORD looketh on the heart." (1 Samuel 16: 7)

Some of these men and women include Abraham, Moses, Esther, King David, Mary the mother of Jesus, Jesus disciples and even Saul who later became the great Apostle Paul.

In some, God saw hearts that were willing to be obedient and faithful to do exactly what God would ask them to do. Some of them God saw Zeal with which the Kingdom of God would be spread. In some He saw contrite and humble hearts. Yet, in others, He saw determination against all odds even risking death because of salvation of God's people.

Another group of people that God used as vessels, actually were willing to follow diligently in the footsteps of their leaders. People that God had placed over them. Those that God gave authority over them, as their leaders. We see that in Joshua who was Moses' servant; Elisha who was prophet Elijah's servant.

Some of the people were fearful, but that did not prevent God from using them, look at Gideon, (Judges 6:36-40, 7:1-25, 8:1-3) or even Prophet Jonah who was fearful to go to deliver God's message to the people of Nineveh.
(Jonah 1:1-17)

So take heart, wherever you are, God is very much willing to use you. Are you serving as a Pastor's armour bearer, ministering to all his needs, be faithful and God will reward you. Elisha, Elijah's servant, got a double portion of Elijah's anointing. Joshua, Moses' minister led the Israelites into the promised land after the latter died.

So, you may be asking, why is it taking God so long to use me then? Well Jesus said, "It is finished." God has done His part. What is remaining, is for you and me to do our part. There are things or characteristics that we have to walk in, in order to position ourselves and to have the right attitude, for God's call upon our lives to manifest.

We have to take the whole counsel of God and walk in it. Try to count how many years the people mentioned above took to walk in their call. Jesus himself was thirty years when he started. Others were much younger. Jeremiah was only a child. David was anointed, but it took time, patience and long suffering for that anointing to manifest. So take heart, your age is not a factor. There are other factors.

Exercises to be done:

Go on a "Fast" for one day. (You may do a liquid fast or a dry fast depends on you, it is the hearts attitude here, that matters). From 6:00 am to 6:00 pm.

As you go about your day, take a pen and paper. Pray at 6:00 am asking God to forgive you all your sins, (Daniel 9:3-20). Ask the Holy Spirit to help you remember every unrepented sins that might be in your life. Any unforgiveness that you might have. Mark 11: 25-26. As they come into remembrance, write them down on the piece of paper.

Be sincere. It is only you and God that know the deep things of your heart, but God knows you even better than yourself, and His Holy Spirit will reveal them to you. The spirit of a man is the candle of the LORD searching the inward parts of the belly. (Proverbs 20:27). Search me, O God, and know my heart: try me, and know my thought: And see if there be any wicked way in me, and lead me in the way everlasting (Psalm 139: 23-24)

Repeat this at 9:00 am, 12:00 pm, 3:00 pm and finish at 6:00 pm. Praying, confessing and writing down all the sins in your life as the Holy Spirit helps you remember them.

At 6:00 pm, as you finish the fast, thank God for forgiving you all your sins.

Then burn this sheet of paper with fire, (Deuteronomy 7:5) and plead the blood of Jesus over you.

The purpose of this is to begin a fresh with God. To be cleansed from all unrighteousness, those sins that you might have forgotten to repent.

Mathew 5:8 says, "Blessed are the **pure** in heart, for they shall see God." And you want to be pure especially now, that you are praying for God's call upon your life. God is Holy and He can not occupy the same place with any other thing.

Then, pray in the Spirit, in your prayer language. Stretch your spiritual muscles and pray.

Notes:

Write exactly how you feel after these exercise. Any revelations. This is a Holy Ghost school so write notes as you receive them.

CHAPTER TWO

The Characteristic needed to walk in your call

A character of Strength and courage:

It is very important to be strong and courageous. This was the first requirement God told Joshua to have; when He called him to take charge after Moses died.

"<u>Be strong</u> and of a <u>good courage</u>: for unto this people shalt thou divide for an inheritance the land which I sware unto their fathers to give them. <u>Only be thou strong and very courageous</u>, that thou mayest observe to do according to all the law, which Moses my servant commanded thee: turn not from it to the right or to the left, that thou mayest prosper whithersoever thou goest. <u>Have not I commanded thee? Be strong and of a good courage</u>; be not afraid, neither be thou dismayed; for the LORD thy God is with thee withersoever thou goest"
(Joshua 1: 5-9.)

Sounds likc these were very vital ingredients for any one God called. Otherwise God could not have emphasized it so much. He actually <u>commanded</u> Joshua to be strong and have <u>good</u> courage. He says; ONLY be strong and very courageous. Could there be courage that is not good. Why is God saying VERY courageous and GOOD courage?

This reflects on the motive behind your courage. Why do you want to walk in that call? Is it for your own glory? Who is your courage glorifying? The courage that Joshua needed; was to be used to divide unto the people, for an inheritance the land which God swore unto their fathers to give them. It was not for Joshua to use for his own gain.

Any courage that is gearcd towards self gain and not service to God and to humankind is not good courage. The Biblc has several examples:

Gehazi, who was Elisha's servant was one of them. After Elisha told Naaman to dip himself seven times into the river Jordan, and he did and was healed of his leprosy. Naaman was grateful and gave gifts to the man of God, but Elisha said:

" As the LORD liveth, before whom I stand, I will receive none." (2Kings 5:16)

"But Gehazi, the servant of Elisha the man of God, said, Behold my master hath spared Naaman this Syrian, in not receiving at his hands what he brought: but as the LORD liveth, I will run after him , and take somewhat of him" (2Kings 5: 20)

This courage is not a good one, because it is pointing to self gain. Although he uses the name of the LORD, he uses it in vain. His reward, he got the leprosy that Naaman had.

In the New Testament we see another example:

In the early church, we see that they were of one accord. And shared all their possession. However, the word of God says:

" But a certain man named Ananias , with his wife Saphira, sold a possession and kept back part of the price, his wife also being privy to it, and brought a certain part , an laid it at the apostle's feet"
(Acts 5:1-2)

The reward, he gave up the ghost. And his wife too, received the same fate. Why, they had a self seeking courage.

So get the intent of your heart in right standing with God.

How will you know that your courage is self seeking? Well, this is what happens. Whenever we are praying for something, before we receive it, there are things that our spirit promises to do when God blesses us. You may say, when God blesses me with a child I will bring him up to serve the Lord.

Or you may say, when God blesses me with wealth, I will give millions to the work of God. Some people keep their vows to God, however, some break it. And so get the negative results. So listen to the Spirit of the LORD within you and do what He tells you. Obedience always brings the blessing.

Remember Abraham, he never held back Isaac, although he was the only son, and both Abraham and Sarah were old, there was no way, in the natural realm, that he saw another possibility, of God's promise being fulfilled with Isaac gone. But he obeyed the voice of God, anyway. He followed the voice of the good shepherd and the voice of a stranger he didn't follow. God still speaks to men, listen to Him.

That voice is in you. Listen to it. And don't reason with it, don't compromise, and don't try to justify your actions, of not doing what the spirit within you is telling you. There is a big reward when you obey. He is still Yahweh Yireh. Be humble and obey.

"Humble yourselves therefore under the mighty hand of God, that He may exalt you in due time." (1 Peter 5 :6)

Why Strength and good Courage?

Why was it so important to posses these two qualities, of strength and good courage. This is due to the task ahead of you. The task ahead of me. God is not calling you for small things. Our God is a BIG GOD. He is the LORD of HOSTS. He does things in a big way.

His ways are not our ways neither His thoughts our thoughts. His ways are Higher than ours ways and His thoughts higher than our thoughts.
(Isaiah 55:8)

He is not calling you to just be the pastor of a small church. He is seeing that congregation growing, so you ought to be well equipped. He sees beyond us. He didn't just call Joseph to be a servant in Potiphar's house, (Gen. 39:1-6). NO, God had BIG things awaiting him in Egypt. He made him second only to Pharaoh, for a reason, to save His people from famine. He wasn't just calling Esther to be the queen, NO, He was placing her there to save the whole of Israel. He was not calling Paul just to preach, but to preach to the Gentiles spread all over. He is not only calling you for that what you think, He has BIG things for you in store.

"For since the beginning of the world men have not heard, nor perceived by the ear, neither hath the eye seen, O God beside thee, what He hath prepared for him that waited for Him."(Isaiah 64:4)

Let us take a look at what tasks all those that God called had to undertake.

Moses had to face pharaoh whom he was running away from. I am sure he needed courage for that. Then he had to lead a people who erred in their heart, tempted God, proved Him and saw His work, <u>and yet</u>, still did not know God's ways for <u>forty years in the wilderness.</u>

> **"Today if you will hear His voice, harden not your heart, as in the provocation, and as in the day of temptation in the wilderness: when our fathers tempted me, proved me, and saw my work. Forty years long was I grieved with this generation, and said it is a people that do err in their heart, and they have not known my ways."**
> **(Psalms 95:7b-10).**

Moses was not only dealing with their spiritual well being but all other natural aspects of a large multitude. Each influencing another. Not forgetting the spiritual battle within such a multitude.

What about David, he had to fight Goliath whom everybody including the king were afraid of.

> **"When Saul and all Israel heard those words of the phillistine, they were dismayed and greatly afraid."**
> **(1 Samuel 17:11).**

Then later he had to fight all the Israelites enemies.

Look at Esther, she risked her life by coming unto the king into the inner court.

> **"All the king's servants, and the people of the king's provinces, do know, that whosoever, whether man or woman, shall come unto the king into the inner court, who is not called, there is one law of his to put him to death, except such to whom the king shall hold out the golden sceptre, that he my live: but I have not been called to come in unto the king these thirty days."**
> **(Esther 4:11)**

You see, God wants you to know that your call is not only for this first step, it is a continuous journey, helping God's people conquer their enemies, being victorious at different levels. It never stops. When you stop, it is time to be with the LORD.

See Elijah's example. When he had killed the 450 prophets of Baal. And Jezebel wanted to kill him. 1 Kings 18: 40. Fear came upon him. He lost that strength and courage. 1Kings 19: 4.

This is no different in the natural realm. The minute one looses his vision, that is the end. There is no purpose for living anymore. When you stop achieving, when you short circuit your ability in God, then you cease to experience more of Him.

What about our Lord Jesus Christ, did he need strength and courage for the task ahead of him? Of course yes, our Lord Jesus Christ needed to be strong and very courageous not only to preach amidst great opposition but also to face his main call of death upon the cross for our redemption.

"And being in an agony He (Christ) prayed <u>more earnestly</u>: and his sweat was as it were great drops of blood falling down to the ground."
(Luke 22:44)

These examples show us that, not all those that God called, possessed the strength nor the courage needed for the call of God upon their lives, initially, neither do you.

If you sometimes feel that you need strength and courage to walk in the call of God upon your life? Take heart, you are not alone. What these men and women of God went through in their time, is no different in our world today. We need **<u>the strength</u>** and **<u>the courage</u>** just like our earlier brethren did, not only for the initial breakthrough into our call but for the continuous walk in that call; and as we grow from glory to glory.

Notice that I have used the article **<u>the,</u>** because this is a special kind of strength and courage than the world knows. This is "the Strength and the Courage" from The Almighty God, El -Shadday.

This is what God is saying to you and me:

"These things I have spoken unto you, that in me ye might have peace. In the world ye shall have tribulation: but be of good cheer; I have overcome the world." (John 16: 33)

Exercises to be done:

When you wake up in the morning, do the following confessions for strength and courage, Jesus said that the words that I speak to you they are life, so confess the word upon your life: Try to personalize these scriptures. Let them be your earnest prayers.

The LORD is my strength and my song, and He is become my salvation: He is my God, and I will prepare Him an habitation; my father's God and I will exalt Him. (Ex. 15:2)

I will love thee, O LORD my strength. The LORD is my rock and my fortress, and my deliverer; my God , my strength. In whom I will trust; my buckler, and the horn of my salvation and my high tower. I will call upon the LORD, who is worthy to be praised: so shall I be saved from mine enemies. (Psalms 18: 1-3)

The LORD is my light and my salvation; whom shall I fear? The LORD is the strength of my life; of whom shall I be afraid? (Psalm 27:1)

GOD is our refuge and strength, a very present help in trouble. Be still and know that I am God: I will be exalted among the heathen, I will be exalted in the earth. (Psalm 46:1& 10)

GOD is the strength of my heart and my portion forever. (Psalm 73: 26b)

Now after the death of Moses the servant of the LORD it came to pass, that the LORD spoke unto Joshua the son of Nun, Moses' minister, saying, Moses my servant is dead; now therefore arise, go over this Jordan, thou, and all this people, unto the land which I do give to them, even to the children of Israel.

Every place that the sole of thy foot shall tread upon, that have I given unto thee, as I said unto Moses. From the wilderness and this Lebanon, even unto the great river, the river Euphrates, all the land of the Hittites, and unto the great sea toward the going down of the sun, shall be thy coast. There shalt not any man be able to stand before thee all the days of thy life; as I was with Moses so I will be with thee: I will not fail thee, nor forsake thee.

Be strong and of a good courage; for unto this people shalt thou divide for an inheritance the land which I sware unto their fathers to give them. Only be thou strong and very courageous, that thou mayest observe to do according to all the law, which Moses my servant commanded thee; turn not from it to the right hand or to the left, that thou mayest prosper whithersoever thou goest.

This book of the law shall not depart out of thy mouth; but thou shalt meditate therein day and night, that thou mayest observe to do according to all that is written therein: for then thou shalt make thy way prosperous, and then thou shalt have good success. Have not I commanded thee? Be strong and of a good courage; be not afraid, neither be thou dismayed: for the LORD thy God is with thee withersoever thou goest. (Joshua 1:1-9)

Pray in the Spirit, in your prayer language. Stretch your spiritual muscles and pray.

Notes:

Write exactly how you feel after these exercise. Any revelations. This is a Holy Ghost school so write notes as you receive them.

CHAPTER THREE

A character of Communion with God in Prayer

How do you acquire this strength and courage? Well, simple , spend more time with God and you will have the strength and the good courage, that God requires of you.

Go into your prayer closet and seek God's face in prayer. He shall strengthen you. He shall send His Angels to give you strength.

Well, is that it, you may ask, YES, if you need to be strengthened and to be bold, then be in communion with the ALMIGHTY GOD consistently. Look at what Jesus did whenever He needed strength and courage, from time to time. He prayed. And when He was in agony, God strengthened Him.

" And there appeared an angel unto Him from heaven, strengthening Him."
(Luke 22:43)

When you spend time in communion with God, your strength will be renewed.

"But they that wait upon the LORD, shall renew their strength, they shall mount up with wings as eagles; they shall run and not be weary; they shall walk and not faint." (Isaiah 40:31)

"Because thou hast made the LORD, which is my refuge, even the most High, thy habitation; …Thou shall tread upon the lion and adder; the young lion and the dragon shall thou trample under feet."
(Psalm 91:9-13)

That sounds like real strength and courage to me. If I can tread on the lion, the adder and even the dragon, I hope however, that you also realize that the treading of the lion and the adder, comes as a result of having done something first. You have to make the Lord your habitation, your home, your house, your dwelling place.

Looking at all these men and women, in the Bible, we find one thing in common. They were men and women who were always in communication with God. That means, they were always in the presence of God.

As Frances J. Roberts in his "Come Away my Beloved" says, They "tarried not for an opportunity to have more time to be alone with the Lord." Today we would say that, they took time to have quality time with God. It didn't matter to them the tasks at hand, they left everything to talk to God through prayer.

They didn't just have a five minutes of a rushed "Our Father who art in heaven," and then a whole day of sitting in front of the TV set watching movie after movie and anything else that came on the screen. Or on the telephone chatting away. NO!! They all prayed to God, underearnestly.

Look at Moses, he went to the mountain to talk to God, not once, often, and he received instructions and directions, even the ten commandments on how to lead the people of God from Egypt into the promised land.

What about David, as a young lad he sang Psalms to God. He was always away with the sheep, meditating and talking to God in Psalms and Hymns. Seeing God as his Shepherd. Comparing how he cared for his father's sheep, to how God cared for him.

Esther, even went further to ask others to help intercede for her in prayer and fasting. She used both the Prayer of Agreement and Intercession prayer. And God gave her the strength and courage to face the king. God gave her favour with the king. And of course it was for the salvation of the people of God, not for personal gain.

We see Daniel the prophet, spending time praying and confessing his sins and those of the Israelites, standing in the gap for God's people. Fasting and praying. And God sent angels, to not only shut the mouth of the Lions but to also bring answers to his prayers. (Daniel 6: 22. 9: 23, 10: 12)

Our Lord Jesus Christ, even separated Himself from His disciples, not once, just to talk to God. Actually before starting His Ministry, He made sure He spent time with God fasting and praying for forty days and forty nights.
(Mathew 4: 1-2)

These men and women, though they left everything and spent time with God, nothing suffered. They were actually victorious. My dear brethren, (Frances J. Roberts adds), "things are of less importance than you think." Stop rushing and always having a busy schedule. You need to actually pray God to help make time for you to be with Him and He will. Take it to the LORD in prayer. Ask and you shall receive.

If you look carefully you will notice that something special usually happened to these people whenever they came from spending time with God.

Their countenance were changed, (Jesus at the configuration.) They had favour with God and thus with man. They had strength, courage and boldness, that people around them never understood. And they were victorious, they overcame.

That will happen to you too. If you spend time with God, you will be strengthened, you will overcome, doors will be opened.

You might be asking, when should I spend time with God for strength and courage? The answer is NOW, before you start walking in your call. Take Jesus' example. Don't wait until you are walking in your call. You can't learn how to spent time with God as a Leader, you should be an example to your followers then.

If you don't do it now, you won't know how to, during your service. You will be getting in that walk without being purged. The results, you won't last long.

Exercises to be done:

Pray the prayers below everyday of your life. Like Kenneth Copeland says, "they will be a spring board that will lead you into" the call of God upon your life.

Please read them aloud so that you can hear them. This will help increase the level of your faith. For "Faith comes by hearing, and hearing by the word of God" Not hearing anything else. Hearing the Word of God, is the ONLY thing that will increase your level of faith. Don't wait to hear the word of God from the preacher, you read your Bible aloud in addition to hearing the preacher.

Also personalize the prayers. You will feel that the scriptures will be more relevant and speaking to you directly. Remember you are praying the unadulterated Word of God. And God says this about His Word,

" For as the rain cometh down, and the snow from heaven, and returneth not thither, but watereth the earth, and maketh it to bring forth and bud, that it may give seed to the sower, and bread to the eater: So shall my word be that goeth forth out of my mouth: it shall not return unto me void, but it shall accomplish that which I please, and it shall prosper in the thing whereto I sent it." (Isaiah 55:10-11)

Jesus said this about the Word of God,

"…the words that I <u>speak</u> unto you, they are spirit, and they are <u>life</u>." (John 6: 63b)

God's word will give <u>life</u> to the call of God upon your life, as you pray. And Jesus is <u>speaking</u> unto you and me in Mark saying,

"Therefore I say unto you, What things soever ye desire, when ye pray, believe that you receive them, and ye shall have them" (Mark 11:24)

As Kenneth Copeland puts it, "So stir up your faith, and pray the word with confidence," knowing that you shall have what you pray, as His word is released from your mouth.

The Lord is my shepherd; I shall not want. He maketh me to lie down in green pastures: He leadeth me beside the still waters. He restoreth my soul: He leadeth me in the paths of righteousness for His name's sake.

Yea, though I walk through the valley of the shadow of death, I will fear no evil: for thou art with me; thy rod and thy staff they comfort me. Thou preparest a table before me in the presence of mine enemies: thou anointest my head with oil; my cup runneth over.

Surely goodness and mercy shall follow me all the days of my life: and I will dwell in the house of the LORD forever.
(Psalms 23: 1-6)

Sing some Praise and worship songs to the Lord.

Pray in the Spirit, in your prayer language. Stretch your spiritual muscles and pray.

Notes:

Write exactly how you feel after these exercise. Any revelations. Remember you are in the school of the Holy Ghost, so write notes as you receive them.

CHAPTER FOUR

A character that seeks The Help of the Holy Ghost:

You may be saying, but I have been praying and nothing happens. My Pastor, Stan Moore of Words of Life says, well that is it. Your prayer should be protecting you from bad things happening to you. However, I know your frustration, you mean, the call of God upon your life is not manifesting <u>yet.</u>

May be you have been saying, they don't allow me to sing in the church. I don't have a position in the church. You may have a list of all the things that are not right with you, to qualify you to walk in your call. Or putting the blame on other people for the delayed manifestation.

It might be family obligations, lack of funds, maybe your spouse who is not saved and won't understand what you are doing. It might be your children, they are still too young.

You might even say that your academic background does not to give you a platform to speak from. You may have no Degree in Theology, or any degree at all for that matter. What when people ask "who is he/she?" and look in the "Who is Who" and you are not listed. Actually, they find out, that you never even went passed high school?

You might be thinking, I just got saved, my passed is still so fresh?

Well, I am here to encourage you by the Word of God. You have a helper more than an academic qualification, more than funds, more than a supportive and understanding spouse. He is the Holy Spirit of the living God dwelling in the inside of you. Just seek ye first the kingdom of God and all its righteousness and all these things shall be added unto you.

Remember the one inside you. Your body is the temple of the Holy Spirit and Greater is He that is <u>in you </u>than he that is in the world.

"A new heart also will I give you, and a <u>new spirit will I put within you</u>: and I will take away the stony heart out of your flesh, and I will give you a heart of flesh. And <u>I will put my spirit within you,</u> and cause you to walk in my statutes, and you shall keep my judgments, and do them." (Ezekiel 36:26-27)

"Moreover, I will make a covenant of peace with them; it shall be an everlasting covenant with them: and I will place them, and multiply them, and will set my <u>sanctuary in the midst of them for evermore.</u> My tabernacle also shall be with them: yea, I will be their God, and they shall be my people." (Ezekiel 37:26-27)

"What? know ye not that <u>your body is the temple of the Holy Ghost</u> which is <u>in you</u>, which ye have of God, and ye are not your own?"
(1 Corinthians 6:19)

Therefore, there is no rock too rough, no valley too low nor mountain too high to climb. And as of you being very newly born again, this is what God is telling you and me in His word, He says, you are a new creature.

"Therefore if any man be in Christ, he is a new creature: old things are passed away; behold all things are become new. And all things are of God, who hath reconciled us to Himself by Jesus Christ, and hath given to us the ministry of reconciliation; To wit, that God was in Christ, reconciling the world unto Himself, not imputing their trespasses unto them; and hath committed unto us the word of reconciliation. Now therefore we are ambassadors for Christ, as though God did beseech you by us; we pray you in Christ's stead, be ye reconciled to God."
For He hath made Him to be sin for us, who knew no sin; that we might be made the righteousness of God in Him."
(2Cor.5:17-21)

So with the help of the Holy Ghost; you can do it. Nothing or no one can stop you but YOU. Remember, God's word says,

"I can do all things through Christ who strengtheneth me."
(Philippians 4:13)

So you may ask, and how does the Holy Spirit help me? How do I know I have the holy Spirit? I don't feel Him sometimes.

Well, the Holy Spirit helps you by interceding to God on your behalf. Jesus Himself had to be anointed by the Holy Spirit before beginning His Ministry. As John the Baptist baptized Him, the spirit came and rested upon Him as a dove. He also confessed this in the synagogue.

"The Spirit of the Lord is upon me because He hath anointed me to preach the gospel to the poor; He hath send me to heal the brokenhearted, to preach deliverance to the captive, and recovering of sight to the blind, to set at liberty them that are bruised. To preach the acceptable year of the Lord."
(Luke 4:18)

You may say, sometimes I just don't feel like praying, I feel tired. The word of God says, stir up the gift of God that is in you. (2 Timothy 1:6) Make a deliberate effort to just start and you will get in to the mood. The Holy Spirit is an expert of helping our infirmities. He is our helper.

Jesus says don't even think beforehand what you are going to say, just depend totally on God, through His Holy Spirit who is Jesus Himself, He will take control. As long as you have been spending time with Him in prayer and supplication.

When my daughter was about seven years old, and was already in the first grade. Whenever I would come from work, she would run to me, as fast as her little legs would carry her, with all her might into my arms.

Now sometimes I would be carrying shopping bags on both hands, struggling under the weight, and you would think that she was seeing that mum's both hands were tied. NO, she was so convinced and confident beyond doubt, that I would hold her. My weight was not her concern.

Now that's the kind of faith God wants us to have in Him.

Well, you can guess what happened. Of course I never let her fall, my mother's instinct had to move in so fast and I would always find a way *just in time* to hold her. God never lets us fall. He holds us just in time.

As I held her, I forgot about the risk she took, to trust me to hold her and just loved her, happy to be home with them, I have two children.

This is the same risk and trust that God is asking us to have toward Him. At some point in the word, God actually allows us to test Him with our finances. He commands us saying:

"Bring ye all the tithes into the storehouse, that there may be meat in my house, and prove me now herewith, saith the LORD of hosts, if I will not open you the windows of heaven, and pour you out a blessing, that there will shall not be room enough to receive it." (Malachi 3: 10)

That means trust Him like a child trusts a parent, with everything.

If we can trust the Holy Spirit so much that we spend more time with Him praying in the Holy Spirit language, we will have done what the teacher does before he/she goes to teach the students, prepare for the lessons. The teacher spends a lot of time in preparation than in the teaching.

In essence this is what it means, I have said it before but I will say it again:
I can not emphasize enough the need to spend time with the Lord and praying both in your language and in spirit, praising and worshipping.

As Frances J. Roberts puts it; "Tarry not for an opportunity to have more time to be alone with the Holy Ghost. Take it though you leave the tasks at hand. Nothing will suffer. Things are of less importance than you think. Your time together with the Holy spirit, is like a garden full of flowers, whereas the time you give to things is as a field full of stale."

You will experience resurrection life and peace; the joy of the Lord will become your strength; and wells of salvation will be opened within you.

How will you know that you have the Holy Spirit? Well, the Holy Spirit comes upon you immediately you receive salvation. The moment you confess the Lord Jesus with your mouth and believe in your heart that God raised him from the dead, you shall be saved, according to Romans 10: 9-10. That is the exact moment that the Holy Spirit enters you. Why, because it is Him who convicts you of your sin in the first place and who also has given you the courage to confess Jesus Christ as Lord.

As for your feeling His presence in you, he says, He will never leave you nor forsake you. You can grieve Him but He is faithful and just to forgive whenever you repent.

Exercises to do:

Confess the word of God. Remember to personalize as much a possible.

The Spirit of the Lord GOD is upon me; because the LORD hath anointed me to preach good tidings unto the meek; He hath sent me to bind up the brokenhearted, to proclaim liberty to the captives, and the opening of the prison to them that are bound;

To proclaim the acceptable year of the LORD, and the day of vengeance of our God; to comfort all that mourn; To appoint unto them that mourn in Zion, to give unto them beauty for ashes the oil of joy for mourning, the garment of praise for the spirit of heaviness; that they might be planting of the LORD, that he might be glorified.

But ye shall be called named the Priests of the LORD; men shall call you the Ministers of our God: ye shall eat the riches of the Gentiles, and in their glory shall ye boast yourselves.

For your shame ye shall have double; and for confusion they shall rejoice in their portion: therefore in their land they shall possess the double: everlasting joy shall be unto them.

For I the LORD love judgment, I hate robbery for burnt offering; and I will direct their work in truth, and I will make an everlasting covenant with them. And their seed shall be known among the Gentiles, and their offspring among the people: all that see them shall acknowledge them, that they are the seed which the LORD hath blessed.

I will greatly rejoice in the LORD, my soul shall be joyful in my God; for He hath clothed me with the garment of salvation, he hath covered me with the robe of righteousness, as a bridegroom decketh himself with ornaments, and as a bride adorneth herself with jewels.

For as the earth bringeth forth her bud, and as the garden causeth the things that are sown in it to spring forth; so the LORD GOD will cause righteousness and praise to spring forth before all the nations.
(Isaiah 61:1-3, 6-11)

Arise, shine; for thy light is come, and the glory of the LORD is risen upon thee. For behold, the darkness shall cover the earth, and gross darkness the people: but the LORD shall arise upon thee, and His glory shall be seen upon thee.

Whereas thou has been forsaken and hated, so that no man went through thee, I will make thee an eternal Excellency, a joy of many generations.

Thou shalt also suck the milk of the Gentiles, and shalt suck the breast of kings: and thou shalt know that I the LORD am thy Saviour and thy Redeemer, the mighty One of Jacob.

For brass I will bring gold, and for iron I will bring silver, and for wood brass, and for stones iron: I will also make thy officers peace, and thine exactors righteousness.

Violence shall no more be heard in thy land, wasting nor destruction within thy boarder; but thou shalt call thy walls salvation, and thy gates Praise.

The sun shall be no more thy light by day; neither for brightness shall the moon give light unto thee: but the LORD shall be unto thee an everlasting light, and thy GOD thy glory.

Thy sun shall no more go down; neither shall thy moon withdraw itself: for the LORD shall be thine everlasting light, and the days of thy mourning shall be ended.

Thy people also shall be all righteous: they shall inherit the land for ever, the branch of my planting, the work of my hands, that I may be glorified.

A little one shall become a thousand, and a small one a strong nation: I the LORD will hasten it in His time. (Isaiah 60: 1-2, 15-22)

Confess what God says about you in His word :

I am God's child	1Pete 1:23
I am forgiven all my sins	Ephesians 1:7
I am a new creature	2 Corinthians 5:17
I am the temple of the Holy Spirit	1 Corinthians 6:19
I am delivered from the power of darkness	Colossians 1:13
I am redeemed from the curse of the law	Galatians 3:13
I am strong in the LORD	Ephesians 6:10
I am holy and without blame before Him	Ephesians 1:4
I am accepted in Christ	Ephesians 1:6
I am blessed	Deut. 28: 1-4
I am a saint	Romans 1:7
I am qualified to share in His inheritance	Colossians 1:2
I am victorious	Revelations 21:7
I am dead to sin	Romans 6:2, 11

I am loved with an everlasting love	Jeremiah 31:3
I am set free	John 8:31-32
I am crucified with Christ	Galatians 2:20
I am alive with Christ	Ephesians 2:5
I am His faithful follower	Ephesians 5:1
I am the light of the world	Mathew 5:14
I am the salt of the world	Mathew 5:13
I am established to the end	1 Corinthians 1:8
I am the righteousness of God through Christ Jesus	2 Corinthians 5:21
I am seated in heavenly places with Christ	Colossians 2:12
I am a partaker of His divine nature	2 Peter 1:4
I am God's workmanship	Ephesians 2:10
I am being changed into His image	Philippians 1:6
I am one in Christ	John 17:21-23
I have all my needs met by God	Philippians 1:6
I have the mind of Christ	1 Corinthians 2:16
I have everlasting life	John 6:47
I have abundant life	John 10:10
I have overcome the world	1 John 5:4
I have the peace of God	Philippians 4:7
I can do all things through Jesus Christ	Philippians 4:13
I posses the greater one in me	1 John 4:4
I press toward the goal	Philippians 3:14
I live by the law of the Holy Spirit	Romans 8:2
I know God's voice	John 10:14
I show forth His Praise	1 Peter 2:9
I always triumph in Christ	2 Corinthians 2:14
I am more than a conqueror	Romans 8:37
I am an Ambassador for Christ	2 Corinthians 5:20
I am beloved of God	1 The. 1:4
I am born of God and the evil one does not touch me	1 John 5:18
I am complete in Christ	Colossians 2:10
I am the apple of my Father's eye	Psalm 17:8
I am free from condemnation	Romans 8:1
I am a disciple of Christ because I have love for others	John 13: 34-35

Pray in the Spirit, in your prayer language. Stretch your spiritual muscles and pray.

Notes:

Write exactly how you feel after these exercise. Especially after knowing who you are in Christ Jesus. That's your position as a blood bought child of God. Right down any revelations you receive. You are in the Holy Ghost school, so write notes as you receive them.

CHAPTER FIVE

Praying the Word

You may be asking how I pray. Where do I get words to pray for so long, as you indicate? When I talk to my friends it is different. I say something and they say something back to me and it flows smoothly. We move from one topic to another without any effort.

Well, that happens too when you communicate with God. It is a two way communication. You may say how?

Here is how:

When you pray the WORD of God, He gives you revelation knowledge. He is talking with you through His word. He might show you how to schedule your appointments. He might give you a revelation on how to furnish your house.

He might open up a way for a job and you will receive a telephone call from your prospective employer. That is because as you are spending time with Him He is moving and shifting things for your good. As you are communicating with Him, God has already done the selection and the interview and you just walk in to possess your possession.

This is because God is involved in everything in your life. Yes, even in those areas you don't think. There is no separating God from anything concerning you. There is nothing that father's do that He can't do, and He is your Father. God's ways are higher than ours and His thoughts higher than our thoughts. Yes, it is a two way communication.

When you pray the WORD of God, the Angels who excel in strength, hearken unto the voice of His Word and bring it to pass; and the Ministers of God do His pleasure. (Psalm 103:20-21)
These Angels, don't hearken (don't respond) to other words. So if you pray long prayers without the WORD of God, the angels didn't hear the command you gave them. Pray the WORD of God. That is the reason; I gave you the scriptures up there to pray every morning.

You say, what about my family and friends. I want to pray for them too. The WORD of God has provision for that too. In Ephesians 1:15-, 3:14- , Colossians 3:16- , 1Thesalonians 5:23 and many more. Paul's letters to the churches can be prayed for family and friends at all times.

Take the example of our LORD Jesus Christ. Whenever He was tempted or any situation arose, He used the WORD saying, it is written. He told the multitude that the WORDS that He spoke to them were given Him by the Father. He challenged the rabbis with the scriptures.

So brethren, be strong in the power of His might. Do the same thing that Our Lord Jesus did. Pray and talk the WORD of God upon your life and upon the call of God on your life.

Jesus said that the WORDS He spoke were life. In Isaiah we read

" For as the rain cometh down, and the snow from heaven, and returneth not thither, but watereth the earth, and maketh it bring forth and bud, that it may give seed to the sower and bread to the eater, So shall my Word be that goeth out of my mouth. It shall not return unto me void. But it shall accomplish that which I please, and it shall prosper in the thing whereto I sent it." (Isaiah 55:10-11)

The Holy spirit led me to connect this to the Word of God in Mark.

"And Jesus answering, saith unto them have faith in God. For verily I say unto you, That whosoever shall say unto this mountain, be thou removed, and be thou cast into the sea; and shall not doubt in his heart, but shall believe that those things which he saith shall come to pass; he shall have whatsoever he saith. Therefore I say unto you, What thing soever you desire, when you pray, believe that you receive them and you shall have them." (Mark 11:22-24)

So do you want the call of God upon you to come to life, then pray the WORD.

Exercises to be done:

Pray these scriptures everyday. Not at your convenience. Make time for God. Seek ye first the Kingdom of God. Give Him the first of your hours in the morning. So as you wake up, pray these prayers. Remember to personalize them. Instead of "thy try saying my, and instead of thee say me"

He that dwelleth in the secret place of the Most High shall abide under the shadow of the Almighty. I will say of the LORD, He is my refuge and my fortress: my God; in Him will I trust. Surely, He shall deliver thee from the snare of the fowler, and from the noisome pestilence. He shall cover thee with his feathers, and under His wings shalt thou trust. His truth shall be thy shield and buckler.

Thou shalt not be afraid for the terror by night; nor for the arrow that flieth by day; nor for the pestilence that walketh in darkness; nor for the destruction that wasteth at noonday. A thousand shall fall at thy side, and ten thousand at thy right hand; but it shall not come nigh thee. Only with thine eyes shalt thou behold and see the reward of the wicked.

Because thou hast made the LORD, which is my refuge, even the most High, my habitation; There shall no evil befall thee, neither shall any plague come near thy dwelling. For He shall give His angels charge over thee, to keep thee in all thy ways. They shall bear thee up in their hands, lest thou dash thy foot against a stone.

Thou shalt tread upon the lion and adder: the young lion and the dragon shalt thou trample under feet. Because he hath set his love upon me, therefore will I deliver him: I will set him on high, because he hath known my name. He shall call upon me, and I will answer him: I will be with him in trouble; I will deliver him, and honour him. With long life will I satisfy him, and shew him my salvation. (Psalm 91: 1-16)

Bless the LORD O my soul; and all that is within me bless His holy name. Bless the LORD, O my soul , and forget not all His benefits: Who forgiveth all thine iniquities; who healeth all thy diseases; Who redeemed thy life from destruction; who crowneth thee with loving kindness and tender mercies; Who satisfieth thy mouth with good things; so that thy youth is renewed like the eagle's.

The LORD executeth righteousness and judgment for all that are oppressed. He made known His ways unto Moses, His acts unto the children of Israel. The LORD is merciful and gracious, slow to anger and plenteous in mercy.

He will not always chide: neither will He keep His anger for ever. He hath not dealt with us after our sins; nor rewarded us according to our iniquities. For as the heaven is high above the earth , so great is His mercy toward them that fear Him. As far as the east is from the west, so far hath He removed our transgressions from us.

Like as a father pitieth his children, so the LORD pitieth them that fear Him. For He knoweth our frame; He remembered that we are dust. As for man, his days are as grass; as a flower of the field, so he flourisheth.. For the wind passeth over it and it is gone; and the place thereof shall know it no more.

But the mercy of the LORD is from everlasting to everlasting upon them that fear Him, and His righteousness unto children's children; To such as keep His covenant, and to those that remember His commandment to do them:

The LORD hath prepared His throne in the heavens; and His kingdom ruleth over all.

Bless the LORD all ye His angels, that excel in strength, that do His commandments, hearkening unto the voice of His word. Bless ye the LORD, all ye His hosts; ye ministers of His, that do His pleasure. Bless the LORD, all His works in all places of His dominion: bless the LORD , O my soul.
(Psalm 103: 1-22)

Sing, O barren, thou that did not bear; break forth into singing, and cry aloud, thou that did not travail with child: for more are the children of the desolate than the children of the married wife, saith the LORD.

Enlarge the place of thy tent, and let them stretch forth the curtains of thine habitations: spare not, lengthen thy cords, and strengthen thy stakes; for thou shall break forth on the right hand and on the left; and thy seed shall inherit the Gentiles, and make the desolate cities to be inhabited.

Fear not; for thou shalt not be ashamed: neither be thou confounded; for thou shalt not be put to shame: for thou shalt forget the shame of thy youth, and shalt not remember the reproach of you widowhood anymore. For thy Maker is thine husband; the LORD of hosts is His name; and thy Redeemer the Holy One of Israel: the GOD of the whole earth shall He be called.

For the LORD hath called thee as a woman forsaken and grieved in spirit, and a wife of youth, when thou wast refused, saith thy God. For a small moment have I forsaken thee; but with great mercies will I gather thee. In a little wrath I hid my face from thee for a moment; but with everlasting kindeness will I have mercy on thee, saith the LORD thy Redeemer.

For this is as the waters of Noah unto me: for as I have sworn that the waters of Noah should no more go over the earth; so have I sworn that I would not be wroth with thee, nor rebuke thee. For the mountains shall depart, and the hills be removed; but my kindness shall not depart from thee, neither shall the covenant of my peace be removed, saith the LORD that hath mercy on thee.

O thou afflicted, tossed with tempest, and not comforted, behold, I will lay thy stones with fair colours, and lay thy foundations with sapphires. And I will make thy windows of agates, and thy gates of carbuncles, and all thy boarders of pleasant stones. And all thy children shall be taught of the LORD; and great shall be the peace of thy children.

In righteousness shalt thou be established: thou shalt be far from oppression; for thou shall not fear: and from terror; for it shall not come near thee. Behold, they shall surely gather together, but not by me: Whosoever shall gather together against thee shall fall for thy sake. Behold, I have created the smith that bloweth the coals in the fire, and that bringeth forth an instrument for his work; and I have created the waster to destroy.

No weapon that is formed against thee shall prosper; and every tongue that shall rise against thee in judgment thou shalt condemn. This is the heritage of the servants of the LORD, and their righteousness is of me, saith the LORD.   (Isaiah 54: 1-17)

Pray for your parents, spouse, children, sisters, brothers, aunts, uncles, neighbours, grand-parents, nieces, nephews, friends and their familes, employer, pastors and all God's Ministers worldwide.

Don't forget the leaders and all those in authority including the president and the politicians, so that we may have peace in the land and be able to worship God freely.

I cease not to give thanks for you, (… Insert their names) making mention of you in my prayers; that the God of our LORD Jesus Christ, the Father of glory may give unto you the spirit of wisdom and revelation in the knowledge of Him: The eyes of your understanding being enlightened; that ye may know what is the hope of His calling, and what is the exceeding greatness of His power to us-ward who believe, according to His mighty power, which He wrought in Christ, when He raised Him from the dead and seated Him at His own right hand in the heavenly places, far above all principality, and power, and might and dominion, and every name that is named, not only in this world but also in that which is to come: And hath put all things under His feet, and gave Him to be the head over all things to the church, which is His body, the fullness of Him that filleth all in all.
(Ephesians 1: 16-23)

For this cause I bow my knees unto the Father of our LORD Jesus Christ, of whom the whole family in heaven and earth is named, that he would grant unto you (…insert names) according to the riches of His glory, to be strengthened with might by His Spirit in the inner man; That Christ may dwell in your hearts by faith; that ye, being rooted and grounded in love, may be able to comprehend with all the saints what is the breadth, and the length, and the depth, and the height; and to know the love of Christ, which passeth knowledge, that ye might be filled with all the fullness of God. Now unto Him that is able to do exceeding abundantly above all that we ask or think, according to the power that worketh in us. Unto Him be glory in the church by Christ Jesus throughout all ages, world without end. Amen.

(Ephesians 3:14-21)

For this cause we also since the day we heard it, do not cease to pray for you (…insert names), and to desire that ye might be filled with the knowledge of His will in all wisdom and spiritual understanding; That ye might walk worthy of the LORD unto all pleasing, being fruitful in every good work, and increasing in the knowledge of God; Strengthened with all might, according to His glorious power, unto all patience and long suffering with joyfulness.

(Colossians 1:9-11)

And (may) the very God of peace sanctify you (… insert names) wholly; and I pray God (that) your whole spirit and soul and body be preserved blameless unto the coming of our LORD Jesus Christ. Faithful is He that calleth you, who also will do it. Amen. (1 Thessalonians 5: 23-24)

Pray in the Spirit, in your prayer language. Stretch your spiritual muscles and pray.

Notes:

Write exactly how you feel after these exercise. Praying for the authority, your family and friends is important. Job 42: 10 says, And God turned the captivity of Job, when he prayed for his friends. Also the LORD gave Job twice as much as he had before.

Write any revelations, as the Holy Ghost gives them to you.

CHAPTER SIX

Prayer in the Holy Spirit Language

Jesus cared so much about His disciples just like parents would care about their children. There is no mother or father who will walk out of the house without some cautious, instructional and loving words to their beloved children.

He told them:

"And, behold, I send the promise of my Father upon you: but tarry ye in the city of Jerusalem, until ye be endued with power from on high."
(Luke 24:49)

This is no different with any parent leaving their children in the house for a while. When I am going out and leaving my children in the house, although they are 19 and 16, I still tell them that I will be back soon. I give them instructions too.

Jesus asked this question;

"If you then being evil know how to give good gifts unto your children, how much more shall your Father which is in heaven give good things to them that ask of Him?" (Mathew 7:11)

And Jesus did just what we would do on behalf of our children. Don't we ask help on behalf of our sons and daughters? That's exactly what Jesus did and is still doing; He said he would pray the Father for us;

"And I will pray the Father, and He shall give you another comforter, that He may abide with you forever. Even the Spirit of truth; whom the world cannot receive because it seeth Him not, neither knoweth Him: but ye know Him for He dwelleth within you and shall be in you. I will not leave you comfortless: <u>I will</u> come to you." (John 14:16-18)

I hope you notice that the last sentence says, "I will come to you," so the Holy Spirit is actually, Jesus Himself in Spirit form so that He can be in all of us at the same time in different places. Helping our infirmities.

My dear brethren, if you are filled with the Holy Ghost with the evidence of speaking in tongues, then this is what Paul says happens:

"Likewise the Spirit also helpeth our infirmities; for <u>we know not</u> what we should pray for as we ought : but the Spirit, Himself maketh intercession for us with groanings which cannot be uttered."
(Romans 8:26)

Did you get that? the Holy Spirit <u>helps our infirmities</u>, for <u>we don't know</u>? And did you get how to pray in the Spirit? Let me just repeat that section.

"but the Spirit, Himself maketh intercession for us with <u>groanings</u> which <u>cannot be uttered</u>."

You just open your mouth, and start praying. He, the Holy Spirit is interceding to God on your behalf. What is so difficult to understand in this scripture? Isn't that not what you do to help your loved ones? do something for them because they cannot? Or is it the fact that those groanings can not be uttered that makes some people so uncomfortable? Well, I tell you what, Paul actually says, it is a mystery.

People are comfortable watching, saying, reading or doing any mystery thing in the natural. However, when it comes to the Spiritual things, they get fidgety. They analyze and question. Well, may God's grace and mercy cover you as long as you are still in doubt accepting the ability of the Holy Spirit. But I pray that He the Holy Spirit reveals these things to persons with questions concerning His help to us.

Paul says, I will pray in my language and also in unknown tongues. That language of the Holy Spirit is in you and me.

You may say, I have been praying in tongues and still I see nothing happening. Let me ask you a question, coming back to quality time. How long do you spend praying in the Spirit? Fives minutes, fifteen minutes. Well, can you time yourself next time? This is what Paul is telling you and me.

"For he that speaketh in an unknown tongue speaketh not unto man but unto God" (I Corinthians 14:2a)

Now that sounds like spending time with God and talking to Him.

Do you always spend five minutes or fifteen minutes with your best friends? Do you only spend time with your friends during daytime or even in the evenings and even at night?

Well, I will tell you something about me and my friends. This is from what my children have told; my children have observed me in the years, each time I have my friends around. This is what they say:

"When Mom and Pamela meet, time stops to exist. They talk all of them at the same time; we wonder whether they understand each other. This they do amidst laughter, loud gospel music or a preaching on the Big Screen TV, Shouting Hallelujah.

They eat and drink till 3:00 in the morning. And when they wake up, it starts all over again like it never stopped. When they telephone each other, you can forget it, if you want to use the phone. One time mom bought a card and talked with Pamela on the phone for five hours.

When they sit in the car together, mom will miss the road because of talking, laughing, singing and all.

Can you imagine having such a great time with God? Nothing else matters but your time with God. Praising Him, Worshipping Him, Praying to Him, and Reading the Word for hours, giving Him your full undivided attention. Wow!!! That feels good.

I never thought I was loud, but one time a neighbour down stairs came and asked me if I could lend her one of my CDs, bringing one of her own. Saying she hears me praising and worshipping. She became my friend to this day.

This is what praying in the Spirit, does to you and me. (And I want to be very specific here and say, unknown tongue, please this is not your indigenous language, this is a tongue unknown to you at that particular moment, other people might know it and be able to interpret it, but not you.)

It gives you joy, peace, tranquility and most of all, the strength and courage, boldness, capability and revelation that you would otherwise not have.

Tell you what, just writing this book is one of those things that happened to me as I spent time with God. I have lots of testimonies of things that have happened to my life because of spending time with God. I have seen rules, laws and regulations not only in organizations but in a land being changed for my sake. Paul says:

"He that speaketh in an unknown tongue edifieth himself."
(I Corinthians 14:4a)

Edify means, to **enlighten:** to improve the morals or knowledge of somebody. It means to "build, construct, instruct," also aedis" building, temple" and facere which was used in the 14th century. It is via French edifier or Latin aedificare which means "make"

Surely, you would want to get some knowledge and be improved before you go and make a fool of yourself in front of a large congregation, won't you? I would.

So, you want to walk in your call? Then build yourself by letting the Holy Spirit build you and make you ready. You are the one who has been delaying. You could be walking in your call by now.

"For if I pray in an unknown tongue, my spirit prayeth, but my understanding is unfruitful."(I Corinthians 14:14)

If you have you been trying to read all the theological books and preparing to walk in your call after getting that Degree? You could complete that degree in Theology and still have no clue what your call is? You may get a job in the church but still not be walking in your call. This is what the word of God says:

"Trust in the Lord with all thine heart and lean not unto thine own understanding."(Proverbs 3:5)

It is time to not only go through Theology but make sure you also go through "Kneeology."

Those who don't believe in Praying in unknown tongues have used some parts of the scriptures in 1 Corinthians 14 to dispute it. Some have said that it is not a must that one should pray in tongues. Well, God has given each one of us a "Free Will." Just like Salvation is a choice that we make, so is the choice to desire to be filled with the Holy Spirit with the evidence of speaking in tongues. We make a decision based on the benefits that we have read or have been preached to, about salvation. Benefits like eternal life, being a child of God and being the righteousness of God in Christ Jesus, and enjoying God's promises. Being partakers of all that God has for those who love, worship and reverence Him. So it is your decision.

Paul has told us the benefits of praying in the Spirit. We talk to God not to man in a mystery. We are edified. From Peter we see that we receive boldness, and the Spirit of the LORD convicts people of their sins and they receive salvation. So brethren, I would encourage you to study the Word of God and pray and God will reveal to you what He has for you. Don't just push God's things away because of doctrines. Spiritual things are personal relationships with God. It is not a group thing. You will face judgment as an individual, not as a group.

We all see the courage that Peter had after being filled with the Holy Spirit. Peter who didn't have the courage to support Jesus during his crucifixion, denied him three times. We see him coming out of that upper room with strength, boldness and courage and clearly telling the people what was happening and not that they were drunk as the people thought. That day he preached and five thousand people were converted.

Mark 16:17 "…they shall speak in new tongues…"

**Paul says; "I thank my God, I speak with tongues more than ye all."
(I Corinthians 14:18)**

Due to Paul's praying in the Spirit, we know that he got the inspiration to write all the Epistles. Giving encouragement to the new converts, guiding them in their new found faith, and edifying them, teaching them. Yet we know that Paul was going through persecution himself, how could he have found a heart to encourage others. Through the Holy Spirit, who strengthened him.

He, the Holy Spirit, will do the same to you and me when we do what Paul tells us. Paul says;

**"Praying <u>always</u> with all prayer and supplication <u>in the spirit</u>, and watching thereunto with all perseverance and supplication for all saints."
(Ephesians 6:18)**

If you read these scriptures carefully, here is what Paul is telling you and me. That if we want to preach or help others that we first have to edify ourselves. Then and only then, can we have the revelation knowledge to go and preach to the congregation. Or walk in any other call that God is calling you on.

Because you have been spending time with God and not with men. Something happens. You get strengthened, you get renewed energy, and you get direction and instructions. You get spiritual guidance; leading to particular scriptures and get a whole new revelation that you never had before. You get favour with God thus favour with mankind. You do things beyond your natural ability. Miracles happen. You get insight. Your countenance changes, you become humble. "Humble yourself under the mighty hand of God and He will exalt thee in due time. You get much more.

Jesus emphasizes the ability of the Holy Spirit by saying;

"But when they shall lead you , and deliver you up, take no thought beforehand what ye shall speak, neither do ye premeditate; but whatsoever shall be given you in that hour, that speak ye, for it is not ye that speaketh, but the Holy Ghost "(Mark 13:11)

Only when you have been spending time with God, praying in the Holy Spirit, can you be able to have such a peace, confidence and trust upon the Holy Spirit; to let the Him take control of your situation. Because you have known Him. You have seen Him at work in your circumstances before. You have experience with Him and so you can be assured that He is able to take care of this one too.

Your prayer life and your life are intertwined. Your life on the natural actually depends on your prayer life. Again, I repeat, don't just give God one hour of your 24 hours. and don't just kneel down, pray and walk off and go. If I would do that to a friend of my, she would ask me if all is fine?

There has to be an exchange taking place during your prayer time. Please just tune yourself to God. Remember God is answering you. There is a give and take process going on. You don't have to be in that one position, you can always be in prayer even as you go about your business. It is your heart's attitude. Be in the prayer mode 24/7. You are the temple of the LORD.

When Daniel was praying, look at how much time he spent in prayers. At first, we find out that his colleagues reported him because he spent time praying. Daniel 6:10 actually says three times a day. You mean in his busy schedule, Daniel actually took time off to spent time with God, because that's what prayer is. And not once, three times a day. Well are you too busy to do that at your work place. This is a challenge to you and me.

Daniel in Daniel 9:3-19. Is praying through all those verses. You may be saying what? in all those verses he was praying, I wonder what he was telling God. However, the point I want to drive home here is the exchange that was taking place as he prayed.

" And whiles I was speaking , and praying , and confessing my sin and the sin of my people Israel and presenting my supplication before the LORD my God for the holy mountain of my God; Yea, whiles I was speaking in prayer, even the man Gabriel, whom I had seen in the vision at the beginning, being caused to fly swiftly, touched me about the time of the evening oblation. And he informed me, and talked with me, and said, O Daniel, I am now come forth to give thee skill and understanding. At the beginning of thy supplications the commandment came forth, and I am come to shew the; the matter ,and consider the vision." (Daniel 9:20-23)

Further down we see that, that exchange can be interfered with in the spiritual realm. However, continual prayer and supplication is important.

"Then said he unto me, fear not, Daniel,: for from the first day that thou didst set thine heart to understand, and to chasten thyself before thy God, thy words were heard, and I am come for thy words. But the prince of the kingdom of Persia withstood me one and twenty days but, lo, Michael, one of the chief princes came to help me, and I remained there with the kings of Persia." (Daniel 10:12-13)

The power of prayer can not be underestimated, When Peter was kept in prison under tight security. King Herod intending to kill him with the sword the way he had just killed John and James. We see God sending an Angel, in answer to the prayer that was made <u>without ceasing</u> by the church, unto God for him. Acts 12:1-19.

Whenever you set your heart to pray, God hears and He sends his Angels to bring your answers. That should make you want to pray every second. Spend time in prayer, actually make your life a prayer life.

Remember, the disciples were to wait until they were endued with the Holy Ghost. Pray to be endued by the Holy Ghost. Otherwise you will be like a soldier going to war without his armour. Remember praying in the Spirit is one of the armaments mentioned in Ephesians 6:18a; praying *always* with all prayer and supplication in the Spirit.

Exercises to be done:

Play Praise and Worship songs as you Pray in the Spirit, in your prayer language. Stretch your spiritual muscles and pray.

Notes:

Write exactly how you feel after these exercises. This is a Holy Ghost school so write notes as you receive them.

CHAPTER SEVEN

Study the Word of God

Students of any profession, usually study in depth and late into the night.

They go into depth researches to discover more and prove their findings. They spend their time in the Laboratories, in the Libraries and presently, behind the computers. Seeking for information. Writing Research papers, Dissertations and Theses.

They become specialists in their various fields of study. Be it Religion, Science, Business, Finance, Arts etc.

As a Christian, you are naturally a student of the Bible. You need to study the Word of God, in depth just like the students of the other fields of knowledge.

However, this is unfortunately not so with most Christians. What do the students of the Word of God do? They can't even study for one hour. They won't even use the concordances and other Bible commentaries, to do reference and find more about the word of God. They won't even have time to attend Bible studies at the Church on Wednesdays. They are encumbered with the cares of the world.

Apostle Paul encourages us to study.

"Study to shew thyself approved unto God, a workman that needeth not to be ashamed, rightly dividing the word of truth." (2 Timothy 2:15)

Peter Daniels one of the World's renown millionaires and speaker, once said, that when asked, if there was a common denominator of all Christians all over the world, irrespective of culture, nationality or denominational background, he says, his answer was FEAR. Well I will add to that and say, LAZINESS.

In as much as most Christians may lack boldness and courage to embark on unknown and unclear Business Projects. They are also lazy to read, study, and meditate upon the word of God. They don't press hard enough.

They don't renew their minds with the word of God. Most of them have been in the church all their lives and have never opened the Bible, they depend on their priests or pastors to read and feed them the word. Yet they want the call of God upon their lives to manifest.

Most of Christians are known as Sunday Christians. They are only church goers.

After everything on Sunday or Saturday, whatever the case may be, they put everything away until the next Sunday/Saturday. What would happen if you saw your child who is a student, never opening their books to study or do assignments after school? I am sure most parents would question them. If you as a Father expect your child to study after school, how much more does your Father in heaven expect you to study His word at home?

Every good student of any field of knowledge, does not depend on his teacher alone but does his homework, reads widely, crams and meditates upon his work to become an expert in his field of specialization. Then and only then, can he authoritatively be able to present anything to his audience.

Our spiritual walk with the Lord is no different.

Exercises to be done:

Start reading the word of God on a daily basis.

In addition to your daily reading of the Bible, read a chapter of the book of Proverbs everyday, for the rest of your life.

Attend your Church's Bible study classes.

Pray in the Spirit, in your prayer language. Stretch your spiritual muscles and pray

Notes:

Write exactly how you feel after these exercises. This is a Holy Ghost school so write notes as you receive any revelations and insights.

CHAPTER EIGHT

Give thanks to God, Praise Him, Give Him Glory due unto His Name; Honour Him; Magnify Him; Worship Him in the Beauty of holiness:

Well, we have seen what happens when we pray. God sends our answers through His holy angels. Now let's see what happens when we Praise God.

The Word of God says that the LORD inhabits the Praises of His people.

Well, to habit does not mean just coming and going. It means living in there, dwelling in there. Our Praises are our God's dwelling, house, home, habitation etc.

Whenever you open your mouth to Praise, God lives in that Praise, He is in that voice and alive, He is in those words. As Christians, we should stop wasting our precious gift, by singing to any other thing but God. If a song does not praise God, then it must be a song of praise to something else. Thou shall not have any other gods beside me says the LORD. I am a jealous God. I do not share my glory with anybody.

"For thou shalt worship no other god: for the LORD, whose name is Jealous, is a jealous God." (Fxodus 34:14)

"I am the LORD: that is my name: and my glory will I not give to another, neither my praise to graven images." (Isaiah 42:8)

Miracles happen whenever we Praise God. In Act 16: 16-40, Paul and Silas were cast in to prison, but while in there, they were praying and singing praises unto God; and the other prisoners heard them.

v. 26 says, And suddenly there was a great earthquake, so that the foundations of the prison were shaken; and immediately all the doors were opened, and every one's bands were loosed.

Could you have been Praising God while in jail? Most of us could have been thinking and worrying instead. Paul and Silas teach us some lessons today. Whatever circumstance that you might be in today, even if it feels like a prison, will fall apart and release you, if you only start spending more time Praising and Worshipping the LORD GOD ALMIGHTY.

When we Praise God, He comes personally to our rescue. He does not send the angels. No, He comes personally because He is dwelling in those Praises. And He does not only rescue us, He rescues all those that are with us. Everyone's bands were loosed. He brings salvation to all, He also gives us favour with Him and therefore favour with mankind. And He makes the world know that we are called by His Name and they are afraid of us.

If you are in a church that does not encourage a lot of singing praises to the LORD, I would encourage you to do more of singing and praising in your home and you will see God move.

Worship is one thing that we just need to do 24/7. In Rev. 4:8-11 says,
And the four beasts had each of them four wings about him, and they were full of eyes within. And they rest not day and night, saying, Holy, holy holy Lord God Almighty, which was, and is and is to come.

"Give unto the LORD the glory due unto His name; bring an offering and come into His courts. O worship the LORD in the beauty of holiness: fear before Him all the earth."
(Psalm 96: 8-9)

When Paul and Silas, were jailed waiting to be charged and executed, they prayed and sang praises to the LORD at night. They sang loud enough, that the word of God says that the other inmates heard.

Those that are of the world are actually very energetic, in the evenings till the wee hours of the morning. They start going to the Discos and other social places around 11:00 pm. And dance to their god till 3:00 am. (I think our God deserves more than that).

However, what do we as Christians do? we go home and sleep. Rebuke that slumbering Spirit and Praise the LORD, Dance to Him, Worship Him and Give Him the Glory due unto Him. Pray in the Spirit with a background praise and worship. Stir up your spirit and have a good time with God, dancing to the LORD. Churches start having all night praise and worship sessions so that the Christian youth can channel all the energy they have in the right place, doing the right thing with the right people and getting the right results, as my Pastor Stan Moore puts it.

In the Old Testament Jehoshaphat, King of Judah and King David were known to Praise and Worship God. And mighty things happened in their lives. Praises actually bring the glory of God upon His temple. Remember you are the temple of the LORD.

"It came even to pass , as the trumpeters and singers were as one, to make

one sound to be heard in praising and thanking the LORD; and when they lifted up their voice with the trumpeters and cymbals and instruments of musick, and praised the LORD saying, For He is good and His mercy endureth for ever: that the house was filled with a cloud , even the house of the LORD; So that the Priests could not stand to minister by reason of the cloud: for the glory of the LORD had filled the house of God." (2 Chronicles 5:13-14)

"And when he had consulted with the people he appointed singers unto the LORD , and that should praise the beauty of holiness, as they went out before the army, and to say, Praise the LORD; for His mercy endureth for ever. And when they begun to sing and to praise, the LORD set ambushments against the children of Ammon, Moab and mount Seir, which had come against Judah, and they were smitten." (2 Chronicle 20:21-22)

From these scriptures we see that when we Praise God, not only does He fill us with His glory, but He also fights our battles. So whatever it is that is blocking your breakthrough of the call of God upon your life, Praise God and He will take care of it. Praise seems to be bringing instantaneous results. That is because God inhabits them. And where the Spirit of the LORD is, there is freedom.

If you want the call of God upon your life to manifest, be a person that praises the LORD. David as a young lad was known for singing and playing his harp. Psalm is full of instructions on how to praise God. Remember, God is not a respecter of persons. David was a King and he praised God. We have big names in the Bible like King Solomon who was the wealthiest and wisest man on earth, he too praised God. No one is too big, too important or too small to sing praises to the LORD.

Whenever you go to church, open you mouth and sing praises to the LORD. Psalm says;

Make a joyful noise unto the LORD all ye lands. (Psalm 100:1). I believe we all know what noise is. So go ahead and make a joyful one to the LORD.

PRAISE ye the LORD, O give thanks unto the LORD; for He is good; and His mercy endureth for ever. (Psalm 106:1)

O CLAP your hands, all ye people; shout unto God with the voice of triumph. (Psalm 47:1)

Sing aloud unto God our strength; make a joyful noise unto the God of Jacob. (Psalm 81:1)

Praise ye the LORD. Praise God in His sanctuary;
Praise Him in the firmament of His power.
Praise Him for His mighty acts.
Praise Him according to His excellent greatness.
Praise Him with the sound of trumpet
Praise Him with the psaltery and harp
Praise Him with tumbrel and dance
Praise Him with stringed instrument and organs
Praise Him upon the loud cymbals
Praise Him upon the high sounding cymbals
Let everything that hath breath Praise the LORD,
Praise ye the LORD. (Psalm 150)

Exercises to be done:

Play Praise and Worship songs everywhere you are. In your car, in your house.

Switch off the TV today and just sing Praises to the LORD in your house. Praise Him, Worship Him, And Give Him Glory.

If you have Praise and Worship DVDs play them.

Let your Praise and Worship ON in the background the whole night.

Read Revelation chapters 4 and 5 everyday.

Buy a note book and start writing everyday, what you receive as you lead a prayerful life and as you become a vessel that praises the LORD.

Notes:

Write exactly how you feel after these exercises. Remember this is a Holy Ghost school so write notes of anything you receive.

CHAPTER NINE

Take the whole Counsel of God:

If you want to walk in your call, don't choose what to take and what not to take from the Word of God. Don't compromise some things just because you want to appeal to a certain group of people.

Some have decided for reasons known to them, to take the New Testament rejecting the Old Testament. Others have accepted the Old Testament, but rejecting the New. Yet others take the Bible as whole, and choose what parts to take and which ones to reject. They all have their justification and arguments for their doctrines.

Some examples of these choices are seen in issues concerning the baptism of the Holy Spirit with the evidence of speaking in unknown tongues, Tithes and offering, the issue of First Fruits, Baptism, and the Holy Communion, Praising the LORD with loud singing and instruments or even the issue of Salvation in Christ Jesus, among others.

The Word of God has this to say about that.

"For I testify unto every man that heareth the words of the prophecy of this book, if any man shall add unto these things, God shall add unto him the plagues that are written in this book; And if any man shall take away from the words of the book of this prophecy, God shall take away his part out of the book of life, and out of the holy city, and from the things which are written in this book." (Revelation 22:18-19)

Others might argue that this only refers to the prophecy in the book of Revelation, however, remember Jesus said, all things shall pass away but His Words shall not pass away.
Jesus also said,

Think not that I am come to destroy the law, or the prophets: I am not come to destroy, but to fulfill." (Mathew 5:17)

Please follow the whole Concept of God, as revealed in His Word. If you are in a church that is not doing it right, the Holy Spirit is your helper, and He will help you, guide and direct you on what to do. The Word of God will guide you.

"Thy word is a lamp unto my feet and a light unto my path"
(Psalm 119:105)

Spend time with Him and He will truly teach you the truth, and the truth shall set you free. (John 8:32). The only way the Holy Spirit will guide you is through the Word of God and by Prayer, earnest prayer.

Some people, may have started walking in any one of the five fold ministries, however, because they never waited to be endued by the Holy Spirit, hence never let the Lord build the house, they never experience much growth. Down the road you don't hear them. They built on sinking sand not upon the Rock of Ages. So make sure it is God's call upon your life, and never move unless He tells you to move. He who started a good work in you is also faithful to accomplish it.

"Except the Lord build the house, they labour in vain that build it."
(Psalm 127:1)

This does not apply only to our spiritual walk; it applies in all walks of life. In our relationships, career choices, Ministry of Helps etc. We all want to be sure God is in whatever we do.

You will know it is of God, because you will find peace. It will be easy for you. You will be motivated. Ideas will keep on coming. Doors will keep on opening up, and one thing will lead to another. The Holy Spirit, your guide will bring things your way. Windows of heaven will open, and floodgates of heaven will open; and as you go along, everything will fall in place.

Are you struggling in your career? Then pray and be sure it is what God wants you to do. Are you struggling in your relationship? Then pray and see what the Holy Spirit is telling you to do about it.

Exercises to be done:

Continue reading the Word of God on a daily basis.

Continue reading a chapter of the book of Proverbs everyday, for the rest of your life.

Attend your Church's Bible study classes.

Continue confessing the prayers under praying for Family and friends.

Continue confessing the prayers under praying the WORD.

Continue Praising and Worshipping.

Continue leaving Praise and worship on the background at night.

Pray in the Spirit, in your prayer language. Stretch your spiritual muscles and pray

Notes:

This is your new lifestyle; Write exactly what you are going through at this point. I encourage you to make notes of any revelations, any difficulties. If you sometimes feel it is too much, don't worry. Keep on. Stretch your spiritual muscles. That is part of purging. You can not be pure silver or gold with all the impurities. And your flesh will cry for attention. This is a Holy Ghost school.

CHAPTER TEN

Always do a personal check

Often time people have labeled any disaster as "an Act of God" well it isn't an act of my "GOD." It may be an act of a "god" but not mine; the god of this world, but not my GOD. This has been a lie that the enemy has designed to destroy the image of GOD in man. God does not require the help of the enemy to correct His children. However, when man disobeys God, he has broken the hedge of protection and is separated from God. He has let the enemy enter into his life and thus the woes of the present world.

The character of GOD shows very well that there is no evil in HIM. He is LOVE. He forgives all our iniquities. He is good. He loved the world so much that He had to get us back to Him no matter what we had done. And He did that by sending His only begotten Son Jesus Christ, that whosoever believes in Him should not perish but have eternal life.

Well, it is always easy to push the blame on someone else, whenever things go wrong. This is not a new thing. Adam pushed the blame not only on Eve, but also on God. He said,

"The woman whom thou gavest to be with me, she gave me of the tree, and I did eat." (Genesis 3:12)

"And the woman said, the serpent beguiled me, and I did eat." (Genesis 3:13b)

So it is not a wonder, that the world will blame the creator for the consequences of their actions. The Word of God says, there is nothing new on the face of the earth. Adam did it and the world still does it. Jesus, the new Adam has come and shown us the character of God. He has compassion for His people. Everywhere Jesus went, He was doing good. A mighty Healer, He cleansed the lepers. When the cripples saw, they started walking. He is the great physician. He raised the dead. He fed the hungry. Jesus is God's righteousness revealed to us. And He is good and good all through.

Well, if anything goes wrong in your life, career, and the call of God on your life, with your house, children, and ministry. Never blame GOD.

Malachi 3:13 says "Your words have been stout against me..." Please never let your words be stout against GOD. He has given you life, hence a chance to repent and turn to Him and enjoy all His promises.

The Bible says, when the hedge is broken, the serpents will bite.

He that diggeth a pit shall fall into it; whoso breaketh an hedge, a serpent will bite him. (Ecclesiastes 10:8)

Many through carelessness break the protective hedge God has placed around their lives, the lives of their loved ones and property. Thus they allow the enemy to destroy them, their families and their property. The good news is that, what is killed, stolen or destroyed by the enemy can be restored by God. Jesus said I am come that you might have life and life more abundantly.
(John 10:10)

God has promised in Joel 2:25 to restore unto us our lost and wasted years. Everything lost to the devil will be restored by God. Job lost all but in the end everything was restored to him even in multiple-fold.

God does not require any help from the enemy to correct us. If anything ever seems wrong, do what I call a "personal check" Look at your house meaning yourself. Is there a door you have opened to the enemy?

It might start with a small little lie, or not paying tithe just once, or not praying before sleeping or in the morning when you wake up or listening to something that grieves the Holy Spirit. A little of what is a normal visit to a friend, or even a gift given by a friend. The list is endless. But the effect of one thing is like a domino effect. If you realize a little sin, please repent immediately to stop that domino effect.

As Christians, we have to be watchful. Satan, like a roaring lion is out seeking whom to devour. Let us not give him any place in our lives. You and me from the day we accepted the Lord Jesus Christ as our Lord and Saviour; we declared war openly against satan. We are making war in the heavenlies.

Everything we do, say, listen to or hear, shows that we are in this world but not of the world. That makes us his targets but take heart; we have overcome him by the Blood of the Lamb and by the word of our testimony.
(Revelation 12:11)

Paul tells us how to fight our battles. Take up your armour, like a good soldier and fight the good fight of faith.

"Finally brethren, be strong in the Lord, and in the power of His might. Put on the whole armour of God that ye may be able to stand against the wiles of the devil. For we wrestle not against flesh and blood, but against principalities, against powers, against the rulers of darkness of this world, against spiritual wickedness in high places. Wherefore take unto you the whole armour of God that ye may be able to withstand in the evil day, and having done all, to stand.

Stand therefore, having your loins girt about with truth, and having on the breastplate of righteousness; and your feet shod with the preparation of the Gospel of Peace. Above all, taking th shield of faith, wherewith ye shall be able to quench all the fiery darts of the wicked. And take the helmet of salvation, and the sword of the spirit, which is the Word of God; Praying always with all prayer and supplication in the spirit, watching there unto with all perseverance and supplication for all saints. (Ephesians 6:10-18)

Exercises to be done:

Ask for forgiveness if your words have been stout against God. (Job 42:1-6)

Praise and worship God.

Pray in both your language and in Spirit.

Notes:

This is your new lifestyle; Write exactly what you are going through at this point. Again you are encouraged to write down any revelations, any difficulties. If you sometimes feel it is too much, don't worry. Keep on. Don't give up. Stretch your spiritual muscles. That is part of purging. You can not be pure silver or gold with all the impurities. And your flesh will cry for attention. This is a Holy Ghost school so write notes as you receive them.

CHAPTER ELEVEN

The Purpose of Your Call:

Whenever God called men or women, it was to use them as vessels to bless His people. To bring salvation from what they were going through at that particular time.

Moses was called to bring the children of Israel from bondage. Samson was called from birth to fight the battles for Israelites against their enemies. King David was anointed to be king in Israel and help them fight their battles, starting with the philistine giant, goliath.

Jesus was called to save mankind from the separation he had with his creator, so that man would again be reconciled to God. Man would once again enjoy fellowship with his creator. Thus enjoy all that comes with that relationship.

My brethren, the call of God upon your life is not for your personal achievement, NO it is for **SERVICE** to His people.

These men and women walked in obedience to the word of God. My pastor, Stan Moore, always says: "Obedience *always* brings the blessing"

When we look from Abraham to Jesus, God called them and placed them at those particular times (dispensation) in order to bless and save His people. To tell the people what God wanted them to do, in order to enter God's rest, by entering into the intended land flowing with milk and honey and to enjoy God's peace and prosperity.

"If my people, which are called by my name, shall humble themselves, and pray, and seek my face, and turn from their wicked ways: then will I hear from heaven and will forgive their sins, and will heal their land." (2 Chronicles 7:14)

We can derive the intent of our own calling from these men and women of the Bible. As mentioned above, they included: Abraham, Noah, Joseph, Moses, Joshua, Samson, Gideon, Esther, David and of course our Lord and Saviour Jesus Christ.

We know that Jesus Christ obeyed God here on the earth as man and not as deity. He was tempted as a man and He rebuked the devil as a man and not as God. He went through the agonies of the cross as a man and not as God. So we count Him among those that showed us how to live in obedience to the Word of God no matter what.

The only powerful thing that we find different from some of us, as compared to these people, is that, they were obedient and faithful despite the circumstances they were in. Faithfulness is a virtue that the body of Christ today needs to learn to walk in. We pray that the Holy Ghost teach us how and help us to be faithful even as our Father is Faithful. Faithful in tithing, in our relationships, in our jobs and having integrity that sets us apart from the world. Taking the whole counsel of God and walking in it, not compromising in some areas to suit our own personal needs. Not doing one thing in the presence of our fellow brethren and another in the company of non-believers. Let us pray the Holy Spirit to help us to be Faithful.

"Likewise the Spirit also helpeth our infirmities…"

"But the Comforter, who is the Holy Ghost, whom the Father will send in my name, He shall teach you all things, and bring all things to your remembrance, whatsoever things I have said unto you." (John 14:26)

Abraham was called for God to <u>bless nations</u> of all the earth through his descendants. Joseph was chosen because Yahweh Yireh (The Lord will provide) saw the need in the future to save <u>His people</u> from famine. Moses was called to save God's people from slavery in Egypt.

**"Come now therefore, and I will send thee unto Pharaoh, that thou mayest bring forth my <u>people</u> the children of Israel out of Egypt."
(Exodus 3:10)**

Joshua was called to lead the <u>children</u> of Israel from the desert or wilderness into the Promised Land. He obeyed God who told him to be courageous and not to be afraid. But to meditate upon the word of God day and night. And then he would have good success. (Joshua 1:1-9)

Samson was born to save <u>Israel</u> from the Philistines. Gideon was called to lead the <u>Israelites</u> to war that was not theirs. The Lord was going to fight for them and only needed a few men as vessels to carry out his plan. (Judges 7:9-15).

You see God does not need our ability. He is able. He only needs an obedient vessel to carry out the mission here on the natural realm. God does not even need the help of diet to use us, as His vessels. Remember Daniel and his friends. They refused to eat the food that was apportioned to them and chose to drink water and eat bread. Yet their countenance looked better than their counterparts.

It is amazing how the things of the Spirit work. The world doesn't just understand it. Today, we would have thought, that they would be malnourished. Or some Christians, would have said, they were fasting meat and wine. Others, would have said, they were on hunger strike, because they had been captured and were in captivity. However, we do know that, that was their everyday meal for that set period of time, before they appeared before the King. Yet they emerged, not only with a beautiful physic but also with wisdom higher than that of their counterparts. How great is our God. **(Daniel 1:9-20)**

David was anointed to be a King over <u>Israel</u>.

"And the LORD said to Samuel, how long wilt thou mourn for Saul, seeing I have rejected him from reigning over Israel? Fill thine horn with oil, and go, I will send thee to Jesse the Bethlehemite: for I have Provided me a king among his sons." (1 Samuel 16:1)

He saved the Israelites from the Philistines during Goliath's time. Again we see that God looks on the inside of a man and not on the physical. God does not need our physical capability; He needs our humble and obedient heart. A heart humble enough to carry out His plans for nations no matter the opposition, the test or the suffering. A heart ready to endure all to death, just to carry out God's call upon their lives. A heart serving God with fear and trembling. Remember because of the Fear of the LORD, David could not cut Saul's head. David's heart is what God saw.

To Samuel, and even to David's father, David was not even counted among those that would be included to an important meeting. When Samuel sanctified Jesse and his sons, (1 Samuel 16:5) David was not even among them. One would wonder, wasn't he a son too. Shouldn't they have called him and had him sanctified too. I wondered when I read verse 1 Samuel 16:10, it says,

"<u>Again</u>, Jesse made seven of his sons to pass before Samuel. And he said unto Jesse, The Lord hath not chosen these." (1 Samuel 16:10)

You mean others could be called in "again", being given a second chance, while others won't even be given a single chance?

Dear brother and sister don't ever worry about it when you feel left out in the church plans or office meetings. When others get several appointments and you don't even have a single appointment. God is on your side. When that happens, do what David did. Keep on doing what you are doing, as long as it is the right thing. Don't murmur. God will pull you out of there with an anointing, so strong they will have to recognize it, for God's Glory.

Esther was placed into the Kings Chambers for that particular time. Again, God, Yahweh Yireh who sees the need ahead and provides for it before hand, knew the intent of Herman's heart, long before Herman himself knew it.

"For the word of God is quick, and powerful, and sharper than any two-edged sword , piercing even to the dividing asunder of soul and spirit, and of the joints and marrow, and is a discerner of the thoughts and intents of the heart. Neither is there any creature that is not manifested in His sight: but all things are naked and opened unto the eyes of Him with whom we have to do. "(Hebrew 4:12-13)

So God placed Esther into the Kingdom **"for such a time as this"**

**Mordecai said to Esther; "For if thou altogether holdest thy peace at this time, then shall there enlargement and deliverance arise to the Jews from another place; but thou and thy father's house shall be destroyed: and who knoweth whether thou art come to the kingdom for such a time as this?"
(Esther 4:14)**

From these examples we can see that there is no greater message than that of salvation, deliverance and being set free from bondage. Whether it was being saved from slavery, captivity, from the enemy in the battle field or from sin or from an enemy's evil plan. The message of salvation is one that brings tears of joy and shouts of triumphant victory to those who receive it, the saints and to the angels above.

Jesus Christ was born to save mankind from sin and reconcile man to God. He was anointed to preach good tidings unto the meek; He was sent to bind up broken hearted, He was to proclaim liberty to the captive, He was to open the prison to them that are bound" He was to proclaim the acceptable year of the LORD, and the day of vengeance of our God. Jesus Was born to comfort all that mourn. He was born to appoint unto them that mourn in Zion. He was born to give unto them beauty for ashes, the oil of joy for mourning, the garment of praise for the spirit of heaviness; that they might be called trees of righteousness, the planting of the LORD, that He might be glorified.

(Isaiah 61:1-3)

And YOU are called, placed at the place where you are, or being told to move to a place; in order to bring deliverance, salvation and freedom to God's people, to the nations, to Israel, to mankind or to His children, in some way, that is known only to God. And He has looked into your heart and known that you can do it. Therefore, don't waste time, get yourself in that position to receive your call today, as you pray, worship, and reverence Him.

Exercises to be done:

Renew your mind with the Word of God.

Praise and worship God.

Pray in both your language and in Spirit.

Notes:

This is your new lifestyle, Write what you are have received. Has your call become clear to you now? Any revelations. Stretch your spiritual muscles. This is a Holy Ghost school, so write everything as you receive them.

CHAPTER TWELVE

Do you feel Inadequate for your Call?

At this point, may be, it has started to come clear to you, what God has called you to do. However, you may be uncomfortable because it might seem too BIG.

Whatever God has called you to do? Do you feel that you are not adequate for that call? If you read the Bible clearly, you will find that many of those that God called felt inadequate; they felt that the tasks were so overwhelming. They even tried to remind God, of their inadequacies, as though He didn't know.

"He that teacheth man knowledge, shall not he know" (Psalms 94:10b)

Take a look at Moses. He thought of how he was not eloquent of speech. I am sure he thought of what a sinner he was after murdering the Egyptian.

Jeremiah said he could not speak well because he was only a child. **(Jeremiah 1:6).**

Jonah even tried running away until the fish swallowed him.

My dear brethren, if you think that you don't qualify to be a vessel because of your lack of education, lack of eloquence in speech or that you are a sinner, I am here to tell you that God's grace is sufficient for you. He says come as you are.

**"God says, Come now and let us reason together, saith the Lord; though your sins be as scarlet, they shall be white as snow; though they be red as crimson they shall be as wool. If ye be <u>willing and obedient</u>, ye shall eat the good of the land.
(Isaiah 1:18-19)**

Let me ask you a question. If your two year old has messed his pampers, does he says oh mummy or daddy, don't pick me up, wait I go and clean myself and then I come to you? No, why? Because this two year old, does not have the ability, to clean himself. So what do you do, you take the baby and clean him or her. Wipe her and change her into clean diapers.

This is the same thing God does to us. Don't wait to clean up yourself, before coming to your daddy God. You don't have the capability to wash your sins, it's by the blood of the Lamb that we enter in, washed and cleansed from all sin, His grace is sufficient for you and for me.

If God was to wait for us to be ready before using us, Paul could not have been used the way he was. If a sinner, Paul was a murderer of Christians. He persecuted them to death. He was called on his way going to do just that.

God will call you and use you in the middle of your sinfulness. All He is looking for is your willingness, drive, courage and desire to obey when He sends you.

Are you waiting for that special crusade or revival, in order to be touched for you to feel and know God is calling you? God is calling you now, in the midst of your busy schedule. Moses was taking care of his father in-laws sheep, David was out taking care of his father's sheep as usual, (David was not even in the revival, if that was to be considered a revival today). Paul was on his mission to persecute Christians.

You know some of us have been in the church too long, and yet God will call people from outside, that will come and answer to God's call and leave us still praying "Oh please God use me, oh God please use me." Stop!!! Stand up and go soldier of Christ. Christ already said "Go ye and preach." God has already mapped out your mission to the end. The things that are impossible to man are possible to God, you know that.

When God called Moses, He told him everything to the end. How Pharaoh was going to refuse to let them go, what God would do and ultimately how and with what, the children of Israel would come out of Egypt.

"And I am sure that the king of Egypt will not let you go, no, not by a mighty hand. And I will stretch out my hand, and smite Egypt with all my wonders which I will do in the midst thereof; and after that he will let you go. And I will give this people favour in the sight of the Egyptians and it shall come to pass that when ye go, ye shall not go empty. But every woman shall borrow of her neighbour, and of her that sojourned in her house, jewels of silver and of gold, and raiment: and ye shall put them upon your sons and upon your daughters; and you shall spoil the Egyptians" (Exodus 3:19-22)

Is this not what happened at the end? Of course we all know this is exactly what happened.

But Moses, even after this assurance still argued and said, **"They will not believe me."** What a faith? At that particular time when Moses was called, his level of faith was where it was. He was going through. He was taking care of his Father in-law's sheep. He was thinking of his past and probably praying never to meet any of those people who knew his past. And now, here comes God, wanting him to face the same people he was running away from. It must have been a taunting idea.

However, this did not deter God. He did not say, "Ok, Moses, I understand." I will send someone else. NO. Neither will God say that to you. My brethren, the work God is calling you for, can only be carried out by you. Are you still giving God excuses on why YOU think you are not qualified for the job? Wake up and take up your call. My call is mine and your call is yours. Your hand will never do the work that is to be done by your eye. We are the body of Christ and fitly joint together, do carry out our respective responsibilities for the Glory of God.

Now, that you've been sitting watching movies on Abraham, Moses, Paul, Jesus or presently by famous preachers like Billy Graham. Do you know that God is making your own movie? Will you let Him make your movie?

Are you afraid like Jonah? You can't run away. Your call is waiting; nobody will be delegated to do it but you. The others have their own responsibilities too. Have you been in that seat for over twenty years? It is time to eat meat and stop drinking milk. Paul says

"For when for the time you ought to be teachers, ye have need that one teach you again which be the first principles of the oracles of God"
(Hebrews 5:12)

Exercises to be done:

Renew your mind with the Word of God.

Praise and worship God.

Pray, both in your language and in Spirit for God to strengthen you and give you clarity and boldness to walk in your call.

Notes:

Write what you are have received. Have you said YES to start walking in your call? Any revelations? Stretch your spiritual muscles. This is a Holy Ghost school, so write everything as you receive them and do what he tells you to do under your pastor, of course.

CHAPTER THIRTEEN

How long should you spend in Prayer

I want you to remember, that we mentioned earlier that Jesus went through the agony of the cross as a man and not as deity. Jesus was obedient to God the Father as human and not as deity.

So, that means, when Jesus was praying at the Mount of Olives, he was human. So how come he prayed for so long each time yet his disciples fell asleep each time? (Mathew 26:38-43)

Prayer is a way of life and part and parcel of your every move. There is no division of your time and prayer.

Ask yourself this question, and answer it truthfully. How long can you pray in your normal language, three minutes, thirty minutes, an hour, three hours?

Well, when the Holy Spirit helps you pray, He helps that infirmity and prays on your behalf and like Paul and Jesus; you will find yourself praying for hours. That way you spend more time with God just as you would spend time chattering away with your friends on a Sunday afternoon after church and then you realize oh, it is 11:00 pm and you wonder how fast time flies away.

Jesus said, Therefore, Watch and pray, that ye enter not into temptation: the spirit indeed is willing, but the flesh is weak. (Mathew 26:41). So let the Holy Spirit help you and you will realize that you are walking in God's call just like that.

In prayer, not only the length is important but also the consistency, the continuity. In Luke 18: 1-8 Jesus talks of a widow who kept on praying the judge to avenge her adversary. And after a while he said within himself,

"…Yet because because this widow troubleth me, I will avenge her, lest by her continual coming she weary me… Shall not God avenge his own elect which cry day and night unto Him, though He bear long with them. I tell you that He will avenge them speedily…" (Luke 18: 4-8)

You can pray in the Spirit in your car, as you shop, the whole day as you go about your business. There is no particular physical position for prayer; it is your heart's attitude. David was praying and praising as he watched his father's sheep.

Exercises to be done:

Pray, both in your language and in Spirit, as you go about your daily business.

Notes:

Have you managed to pray for one, two or three hours? Did the Holy Spirit wake you up in the night to pray? Any revelations? any experiences and testimonies? Stretch your spiritual muscles. Write everything as you receive them. Continue doing what you receive to do. Talk to your pastor.

CHAPTER FOURTEEN

Should you pray aloud or in your heart in the spirit?

I have been asked in several occasions in which language I think before I talk. This is because I speak several languages.

Now, this shows me that unless I speak, no one knows exactly which language I am thinking in. So when we pray silently in the Spirit no one knows whether we are actually praying in English or in the Spirit. So it only becomes obvious in what language we are praying when we open our mouth and pray aloud.

We are not praying for anyone to hear us, however, the spiritual realm hears us. Don't be like the Pharisees who prayed exalting himself, but rather as the publican, humbling yourself before the LORD and He will exalt you.
    (Luke 18:10-14)

We are praying loud' so that the spiritual world hears us. We are declaring war in the heavenlies openly with our loud prayers, and telling the spirits of darkness, so they will know where we stand, we are the people of God called by His Name. and bought by the Blood of the Lamb, Jesus the Son.

(For the weapons of our warfare are not carnal, but mighty through God to the pulling down of strongholds ;) Casting down imaginations, and every high thing that exalteth itself against the knowledge of God, and bringing into captivity every thought to the obedience of Christ." (2Corinthians 10:4)

Now depending on where you are, you will either murmur silently under your breath or just pray loud. If I am in my prayer closet alone I pray loud, and sing loud in the spirit. If I am in a waiting room, I will murmur under my breath. When I am in my car driving I will pray aloud as I play my gospel music. You want God's call upon your life, this is a good starting point, and don't stop. God will begin to move you from one level to the next. He is faithful, if you wait upon Him He will indeed answer you, and He will use you as He will. Amen.

Exercises to be done:

Pray the Rhema Word of God loud, both in your language and in Spirit.

Praise God aloud. Worship Him aloud. In your house or in your car and in the church.

Notes:

This is your new lifestyle, Write what you are receiving. Have you managed to pray for one, two or three hours? Did the Holy Spirit wake you up in the night to pray? Have you had any experiences, discouragements and testimonies? Stretch your spiritual muscles. This is a Holy Ghost school,

CHAPTER FIFTEEN

Die to self

Jesus said, unless a seed dies, it can not produce fruits.

"Verily, Verily I say unto you, except a corn of wheat fall into the ground and die, it abideth alone: but if it die, it bringeth forth fruit. He that loveth his life shall lose it; and he that hateth his life in this world shall keep it unto life eternal." (John 12:24-25)

This is something that all Christians, must deal with. Are you easily hurt by people's words, or their actions? Do you get angry and full of wrath over trivial matters? Do you tend to blow things out of proportion and start strife? It is only the flesh. You have to live beyond the flesh. You have to live beyond the self pity partying. You have to live beyond your ego and pride. You can not be anointed and be angry at the same time.

If you find yourself getting hurt, please pray God to deliver you. Anger will make you not enter the Promised Land.

Moses was provoked to anger by the children of Israel and he reacted to this anger. The repercussions were great; he could not enter the Promised Land. But because of God's grace, He allowed him to see it. There is no justification whatsoever for anger and wrath, no matter what someone has done to you.

Proverbs 29:22 says that "An angry man stirreth up strife and a furious man abounded in transgression."

Wrath (anger) and strife are among the manifestations of the works of the flesh mentioned in Galatians 5:12-21. So don't let yourself miss your call because of it. Repent of anger wrath and strife right now.

Paul says, "… let not the sun go down upon your wrath…"(Ephesians 4: 26) He adds in verse 31, Let all bitterness, and wrath and anger … be put away from you.

All these Bible characters went through a lot, that if they were pity partying, there would be no bible today. However, no matter the persecutions, they forgot themselves and always encouraged others. Look at what Paul went through in 2Corinthians 11:24-28. Again, your call is for service to the people. Jesus had compassion on people and never thought about himself. Abraham never thought of himself but let Lot his nephew take the best part of the land. Die to self.

Exercises to be done:

Pray that God delivers you from all anger and wrath.

Pray both in your language and in Spirit.

Notes:

Write what you are have received. Make deliberate efforts not to get hurt no matter what you hear or see. Especially with your children, spouse or those under your authority. Stretch your spiritual muscles and pray some more.   And remember to listen to the Holy Ghost, and write everything as you receive them. And do what He tells you to do.

CHAPTER SIXTEEN

Renew your mind with the word of God

Mathew 12:34 "Out of the fullness, the mouth speaketh."

If I meet someone, it takes five minutes to know what is in that person. As a man thinkest so is he. But you will only think of what you have been inputting in you. They say in the computer language, "garbage in garbage out"

If I take a bottle and filled it with water, I sure will not expect to pour some orange juice out of that bottle. I will definitely pour out of it just the water I filled it with.

However, if for some reason, I buy margarine, after I use the content, the container will still have that label saying margarine. If someone opens that container, they will be disappointed because they won't find any margarine in it.

Most Christians have become like this empty disappointing container with no margarine in it, in spite of the label they bear. Please, make sure that you are full of the Christ, because He is the WORD of God, so that you are rightly labeled as a Christian with Christ -the Word of God in you.

Jesus was disappointed when he went to the fig tree and found no figs thereon. He cast the tree. Mark 11:12-14, 20-21.

It is important to have the word of God in you, so that those that are hungry and thirsty can come and find spiritual nourishment. Otherwise, you will be cursed.

How do you fill or get the Word inside you? Read the word of God. That means, "Renewing your mind." Why "re-new," Anytime "Re" is used it means that you keep on going to get some more. Re-fill. Or Re-establish. Don't just read it once and say that's it. No. Re-read, thus renew your mind.

Do you go for a fruit punch refill at the food court, the same way, go for a refill for the Word of God, for prayer, for praise and worship? This is your spiritual food. Don't they say, "Never skip a meal?" Well, never skip a spiritual meal, either. Make sure you have spiritual breakfast, a ten o'clock spiritual snack, a spiritual lunch at 12:00, a three o'clock spiritual snack and a spiritual dinner.

They actually say, breakfast like a King. Well, have a morning Glory with God's word. Praising Him in the morning before you leave your house. "The psalmist says,

"Give ear to my words oh Lord, consider my meditation, hearken unto the voice of my cry, my King and my God, for unto will I pray, my voice shalt thou hear in the **morning**, Oh LORD in the **morning will I lift** **my prayer unto thee and will look up**." (Psalm 5:1-3)

Exercises to be done:

Continue reading the Word of God on a daily basis.

Continue reading a chapter of the book of Proverbs everyday, for the rest of your life.

Attend your Church's Bible study classes.

Continue confessing the prayers under praying for Family and friends.

Continue confessing the prayers under praying the WORD.

Continue Praising and Worshipping.

Continue leaving Praise and worship on the background at night.

Pray in the Spirit, in your prayer language. Stretch your spiritual muscles and pray

Notes:

Write what you are have received so far. Stretch your spiritual muscles and let the Holy Spirit guide you in your reading of the Word. Pray some more.   And remember to listen to the Holy Ghost, and write everything as you receive them.

CHAPTER SEVENTEEN

Training Years are never wasted Years

Never despise your training days. Just like we have on the job training or apprenticeship, in the natural, we have it in the spiritual things too. These are your training years. Don't despise them; learn from the experiences you encounter for your future success.

I hope you noticed that it is not training <u>days</u> but <u>years</u>. To be qualified for any position, employers usually look for <u>years</u> of training, was it a four year degree, or a one year degree? Then they look at the years of experience. Most employers want at least three years of working experience. Actually, they even contact your references to get not only your viewpoint but also of those that have worked with you.

It is no different in the spiritual things. Your years of training under a spiritual leader. A pastor or an Apostle are very valuable.

Jesus' disciples were with Him three years. He sent them out not once but twice. In Luke 9:1 and again in Luke 10:1, to let them have a feel of how they would be going out to preach the kingdom of God..

He gave the power and authority. He gave them instructions: take nothing for your journey...etc. When they came back to give a report, they had done a great job. However down in, the disciple John reveals a mistake they did.

"Master, we saw one casting devils in thy name; and we forbade him, because he followed not with us." (Luke 9:49). Jesus corrected them.
"Forbid him not: for he that is not against us is for us." (v. 50)

Christians, we should learn something here and stop the division that is so rampant in Christianity. We are all at different levels of faith; our religious affiliation should not make us loose our call as the Body of Christ.

Paul says, "I have planted, Apollos watered; but God giveth the increase... for we are laborers together with God...But let every man take heed how he buildeth thereupon." (1Corinthians 3:6-10).

Do you take offense whenever your pastor corrects you. Well, I used to. I remember one time I had not been paying tithes in my church for sometime.

The enemy had convinced me that I couldn't pay it. He gave me all the reasons not to. I was a single mom, and so on. We all know his lies.

I had been paying tithe and following the whole counsel of God, when suddenly, I left a door open to the enemy. I had a relationship that was not right. So things started happening. (Remember the "Do a Personal Check" Chapter.) All of a sudden, it became a burden to give God His tithes, it became a burden to attend the staff meetings, I went late to church and missed the morning prayers, and I started questioning - remember the sin in the Garden of Eden? Sin will bring knowledge **that question.**

Well, I thank God for having provided a Pastor who was faithful and obedient to His call. One time I never attended a staff meeting. So the next day- Sunday, I was informed that they had relieved me of my duties as a Bookstore manager until I got myself to pay tithe.

Now, that is what the Associate Pastor said, I am sure God had revealed to His servants, the Senior Pastor and the Associate Pastor more than they said.

Well, I was rebellious. I felt hurt. At one point, I even refused to hug my pastor. (I had not died to self). However, I knew better, not to bad mouth my pastors, not to murmur. I had been taught well. Remember, to whom much is given much is required (Luke 12:48); and because of God's call upon your life, much will be required of you.

Anyhow, I never stopped going to Church, thank God for that. I prayed and repented the sin out of my life. I went for counseling with the Pastor. Note what I said, I repented the sin out of my life. I turned away from that sin, stopped that relationship and rebuked it out of my life in the mighty Name of Jesus Christ. Was it easy? NO. But I thank God, the WORD of God in me was deep-rooted, enough to know that I needed God not man.

Sometimes to break a relationship like that will be difficult; especially if you are a single person and you think this is the right person. He may treat be treating you so well, (Ladies you know the gentleman who opens the car for you) he likes your children and things just seem right. He has a very well paying job and a house too. Wow!!! That just adds cream to the cake. But watch out, the enemy usually sends a counterfeit just before your breakthrough.

If you take a good look at it, there will be loopholes. He does not come to your church. He is spiritual but a different kind of spiritualism. He may invite you there, but listen to the Holy Spirit within you; if the Holy Spirit within you is grieved, then that tells you to back off.

In my case, he was actually in a yoga kind of thing. Well, the enemy will tell you, you can change him. Nope!!! Remember, it is harder to pull someone to the top of a table than to be pulled down. The other thing is that he was married and claimed that their marriage was not working. To give you false hope. The enemy will do that. Give you false hope. He is a liar and that's his specialty. Well, he is doing what he is known for, are we doing what we are known for as Christians?

Well it took sometime, but I started paying my tithes again; it took time, and God is Faithful and just to forgive us our sins, when we repent.

I later became the Pastor's Armour Bearer. You see, the enemy had peeped into my promotion, and he used an area where I was weak, to get my promotion away from me. delaying it. Don't let him delay or take away your promotion or even delay the call of God upon your life. Remember the kingdom of God suffers violence and the violent take it by force. You may just have to swallow your pride and brace yourself for a battle to take up that call of God back from the enemy in Jesus Mighty Name.

God will correct us. You can not be in a position of leadership and have doors open to the enemy. Remember whenever Kings sinned, God rejected them and chose other Kings in their stead unless they repented.

Could it be that a door that you have left open innocently has brought a whole lot of other sins in your life and therefore preventing you from walking in God's call upon your life? Well, repent quickly, there is no one you are fooling but yourself. Paul says this,

" **Be not deceived, God is not mocked: for whatsoever a man soweth, that shall he also reap. For he that soweth to his flesh shall of the flesh reap corruption; but he that soweth to the Spirit shall of the Spirit reap life**

everlasting. And let us not be weary in well doing: for in due season we shall reap, if we faint not." (Galatians 6:7-9)

Exercises to be done:

Volunteer at your church. Be diligent in serving your leader. David's men were with him even in the caves in Adullam. (1Samuel 22:1-2)

Stretch yourself in service to God's servant. Blessings flow from the head down. When your leader is taken care of, you will be taken care of too.

Read books on Ministry of Helps. Books like God's Armour bearer etc.

Declare the scriptures below:

Behold, happy is the man whom God correcteth; therefore despise not thou the chastening of the Almighty. (Job 5:17)

My son, despise not the chastening of the LORD; neither be weary of his correction; for whom the LORD loveth he correcteth; even as a father the son in whom he delighted.

Pray in the Spirit.

Notes:

Write your experiences as you serve the LORD under your Pastor.
Write what your experiences are as you put your hands on the things of God.
Has got placed His hand upon your things? Do you find joy in serving God?
Stretch your spiritual muscles and let the Holy Spirit give you the strength to
keep on serving in Him. As you serve, write the miracles and the challenges
you receive in your life. Write any other revelations as the Holy Spirit
gives them to you.

CHAPTER EIGHTEEN

Never despise humble beginnings

Start from where you are. From now on, take your work as though you are doing it as unto God and not as unto man. Start treating your job as training towards your main call. You will need all those skills you are using at your office or at your job in your call. God will call you from wherever you are serving. Moses got all his leadership training under Pharaoh not in a synagogue. So wherever you are, God has placed that man or woman over you for a purpose. Acquire those skills for your future call.

Remember the servants with the five talents, two talents and one talent.

Trade with your talents wisely and bear more fruit, and God will say, Well-done good and faithful servant; thou has been faithful over a few things, I will make thee ruler over many things, enter thou into the joy of thy lord.
(Mathew 25:15-30)

Are you in the Ministry of helps at your church? Cleaning the sanctuary or are you probably cleaning the bathrooms, clean whatever area, as though it was Jesus cleaning a soul and leading them to salvation, washed by the Blood of Lamb. _

Are you teaching the children? That is a very honourable job. Those are the future Apostles, Prophets, Evangelists, Teachers and Pastors. Moses' foundation was laid from her mother's teachings as she nursed him. Those early teachings will not only be engraved in those children's hearts; but they will mold them into their call; and remember, the Kingdom of God is theirs.

Exercises to be done:

Continue reading the Word of God on a daily basis.

Continue reading a chapter of the book of Proverbs everyday, for the rest of your life.

Attend your Church's Bible study classes.

Continue confessing the prayers under praying for Family and friends.

Continue confessing the prayers under praying the WORD.

Continue Praising and Worshipping.

Continue leaving Praise and worship on the background at night.

Pray in the Spirit, in your prayer language. Stretch your spiritual muscles and pray

Notes:

Write your experience as you change your attitude towards your present work. Stretch your spiritual muscles and let the Holy Spirit guide you in your relationship with your boss. Pray some more, read the Word some more. And remember to listen to the Holy Ghost, and write everything as you receive them.

CHAPTER NINETEEN

Check your love walk

God is love.

Paul tells the Corinthians, that no matter what he does, if he does not have love, it profits him not.

John says, "If a man say, I love God, and hateth his brother, he is a liar: for he that loveth not his brother whom he hath seen, how can he love God whom he hath not seen?" (1 John 4:20)

When Jesus walked on this earth, He had compassion on the crowd. That is why He even cried to God to forgive those who crucified Him. He said they did not know what they were doing.

Dear brethren, if you don't have love for God's people, then you may do everything above, but will never experience God' call upon your life.

It is actually a commandment. When Jesus was asked which one is the greatest commandment He said, Thou shall love the Lord your God with all your heart, and with all your soul and with all your mind. And the second one is like it. Thou shall love your neighbour as yourself. (Mathew 22:37-39) And of course we know the story of the Good Samaritan, when asked who our neighbour actually is.

Jesus asked Peter three times, Simon Peter do you love me? Peter answered and said "Yes my Lord, I do Love you." And Jesus said, "Then take care of my sheep."

Jesus asked Peter the second time, Simon Peter do you love me? Peter answered and said "Yes my Lord, I do Love you." And Jesus said, "Then take care of my sheep."

Jesus asked again, the third time, Simon Peter do you really love me? Peter answered and said "Yes my Lord, I do Love you." And Jesus said, "Then take care of my sheep."(John 21:15-17)

You see, there is no way you can take care of the Lord's sheep without love. Your love walk and your compassion towards God's children should be foremost in your heart. And love is contagious; it will flow from the head down.

Just like a parent can not trust anyone with their children unless they have love for them, Jesus could not just leave His sheep, the humankind, without being sure of the love of His disciple Peter. Our Peter today are the Pastors who take care of the sheep. Without love it is hard to be a shepherd. So just pray for the Holy Spirit to shed abroad His love in your heart to love people especially those that make it difficult for you to love them. Joseph loved his brothers despite all they did to him and sold him into slavery in Egypt.

Exercises to be done:

Pray this everyday:

God I asked you to shed abroad your love in my heart. that I may have compassion upon your people. That I may have love in my heart just like you have loved me.

For God so loved the world that He gave his only begotten Son, that whosoever believeth in Him, should not perish but have eternal life.
(John 3:16)

Though I speak with tongues of men and of angels, and have no love, I am become as sounding brass, or a tinkling cymbal. And though I have the gift of prophecy, and understand all mysteries, and all knowledge; and though I have all faith, so that I could remove mountains, and have no love, I am nothing. And though I bestow all my goods to feed the poor, and though I give my body to be burned, ands have not love, it profiteth me nothing.

Love suffereth long, and is kind; love envieth not, love vaunted not itself, is not puffed up. Doth not behave itself unseemingly, seeketh not her own, is not easily provoked, thinketh not evil. Rejoiceth not in iniquity, but rejoiceth in the truth; Beareth all things, believeth all things, hopeth all things, endureth all things. Love never faileth: but whether there be prophesies, they shall fail; whether there be tongues, they shall cease; whether there be knowledge, it shall vanish away. …And now abideth faith, hope and love, these three, but the greatest of these is Love. (1Corinthians 13: 1-8, 13)

Father I know that a negative attitude toward others can never bring me success. I ask for forgiveness of any negative thoughts I have had on any one. Help me Father God to eliminate hatred, envy, jealous, selfishness and cynicism. Help me Father God to develop love for all humanity in Jesus Name.

Pray in the Spirit, in your prayer language.

Notes:

Make deliberate steps to love people. Write what your experiences. Stretch your spiritual muscles and let the Holy Spirit guide you in your love walk. Try not to bad mouth anyone. And remember to listen to the Holy Ghost, and write anything you receive.

CHAPTER TWENTY

Tithes and offerings; First fruits of all your increase:

So many books have been written about tithing, I would encourage you to read them.

In tithing God allows us to prove Him and see if He will not open the windows of Heaven and pour out a blessing that we will not have enough room to receive. He will also destroy the devourer for our sakes. Our fields shall not yield its fruits before time. And all nations shall call us blessed. In the Bible, there is a specific amount specified to be returned unto God. He says, a tenth of all your income.

Now, offering is that which you thank God with; for what He has done for you. This is your heart's gratitude to God. When people do good to us, we say thank you and sometimes buy them gifts, to show our gratitude. In the Bible, there is no amount specified for offering. It is usually indicated as the best of what you have. It is also shown as a heart's attitude as opposed to the amount. God loves a cheerful giver. In (Luke 21:1-4) Jesus said, the widow gave more than all the other people, she gave all she had, while others gave out of their abundance.

Whereas in tithing God, is the one we are putting to test; in Offering, God is putting us to test. How much can He trust us with His riches? Are we good stewards of His money? We see God testing Abraham when He asks Him to offer His only son Isaac.

The Bible commands us to bring back what is God's as concerning tithes. If we don't, it states that we are robbing God both in tithes and offerings, the Bible says, God loves a cheerful giver. In offering we are giving we are not returning.

Concerning offering, we know from Cain and Abel, that God may or may not accept an offering. So you want to be sure that God is happy with your offering.

Jesus said, give unto Caesar what is Caesar's and to God what is God's. In today's world if one does not pay taxes, he faces grievous charges. If in the natural, one gets punished for not giving the government its due, what do you think happens in the spiritual realm, when we don't give unto God what is due unto Him?

Tithes are actually not ours at all. It is the tenth of all your income. It does not only refer to your basic salary, plus the allowances, it refers also, in addition to these, and any other blessing that God blesses you with.

God blesses us in many ways. If a friend, or your parent, or your employer happens to bless you with twenty dollars, then two dollars out of that, is not yours. It is a tenth of anything coming in your hands.

Whereas in tithing all windows of Heaven are open, meaning we are blessed in all areas of our lives, in offering we get back what we have sowed. If you sow sparingly, you shall reap sparingly, and if you sow bountiful, you shall reap bountifully. In offering, we reap after its kind. So if you want to reap finances, then sow money. If you want love then, sow love. If you want a house then help sow in a house. If you want clothes, then sow clothes. If you want praise then, starting praising people and have good words for people and it will come back to you. If you find that people always put you down and talk negative things to you, then check what words you've been saying or thinking about other people. Most probably you think the same towards other, hence your harvest.

In offering the Bible says, Give and it will come back to you. Good measure pressed down, shaken together and running over, shall men give unto your bosom.

If a farmer wanted to reap a big harvest, He plants seeds in the whole farm. If he however, plants only a single line, he will not expect to reap from the whole farm but only that single line.

Reaping comes in due season, if we don't faint, (Galatians 6:9). It would be outrageous for a farmer to plant his seed today and walk in the farm the next day expecting to see the harvest. Yet many Christian's do expect the harvest immediately; and then when they don't get what they expect, their words become stout against God. In doing so they uproot all what they had sown.

Let this become your lifestyle because, today you are living or reaping, what you have sown in the past years. So go ahead and keep on sowing good seed, so that your life continues to be full of good harvest. If you don't like what you are living or reaping now, you have a chance to change it. Make a decision right away, and start sowing good seeds. It truly comes back in God's time. In His time, He makes all things beautiful. Amen.

We are to give the offering and the first fruit to the Priest. According to Deuteronomy 18: 1-4, the Priest, who was a Levite had no part in the inheritance, but his due was the offerings and the first fruits that the people brought. Today the enemy has attacked the Body of Christ in this area, so much so that, it has kept the body of Christ in poverty.

People have argued about what is being done with the money in the church and there arise a lot of disputes. However, when they go to work, to earn their living, and expect to have a good preaching on Sunday, they never think of how the Pastor spent time preparing for that Sermon. If your Pastor is full time employed, what time does he have to minister to the sheep? It is high time that we stopped muzzling the ox that treadeth out the corn, for the labourer is worthy of his reward. (1Timothy 5:18).

Exercises to be done:

Pray these prayers everyday:

Bring ye all the tithes into the storehouse, that there may be meat in My house, and try Me now herewith, says the Lord of hosts, if I will not open for you the windows of heaven and pour you out a blessing that there will not be room enough to receive it. And I will rebuke the devourer for your sakes.
(Malachi 3:10-11)

While the earth remains, seedtime and harvest … shall not cease.
(Genesis 8:22)

Honour the Lord with your possession and with the first fruits of all your increase; so your barns will be filled with plenty, and your vats will overflow with new wine.
(Proverbs 3:9-10)

Now He who supplies seed to the sower, and bread for food, supply and multiply the seed you have sown and increase the fruits of your righteousness. (2Corinthians 9:10)

Do not be deceived, God is not mocked; for whatever a man sows, that he will also reap. (Galatians 6:7)

If the First fruit be holy, the lump is also holy.
(Romans 11:16)

Give and it will be given unto you: good measure, pressed down, shaken together, and running over…For with the same measure that you use, it will be measured back to you. (Luke 6:38)

He who sows sparingly shall also reap sparingly, and he who sows bountifully shall also reap bountifully. So let each one give as he purposes in his heart, not grudgingly or of necessity; for God loves a cheerful giver. And God is able to make all grace abound toward you, that you, always having all sufficiency in all things, may have an abundance for every good work.

(2 Corinthians 9:6-8)

Notes:

Write what you are have received. Stretch your spiritual muscles and let the Holy Spirit guide you in your giving. As you give write the miracles you receive in your life. Write any other revelations as the Holy Spirit give them to you.

A Lifestyle of Fasting:

Fasting is an integral part of our walk with God. In the word of God, most of the time we find that whenever people were faced with a difficult situation, they fasted and prayed.

In the Old Testament we know Israel was called to help fast and pray for God to hearken unto Esther's prayer before going to appear before the King.

Daniel was always fasting and praying.

In the New Testament, Jesus fasted and prayed forty nights and forty nights before starting His life Ministry.

It is obvious that fasting, was often practiced by the Pharisees and their followers, and even John the Baptist' disciples. In the gospel of Mathew they ask Jesus why His disciples don't fast.

"Then came to Him the disciples of John, saying, why do we and the Pharisees fast oft, but thy disciples fast not?" Mathew 9:14

When, Jesus came back, from the mountains, where the transfiguration took place. A man cried to Him to heal his son. He had brought his son to Jesus' disciples but they could not heal him. Later when Jesus' disciples asked why they could not heal him, Jesus said,

"…Howbeit this kind goeth not out but by prayer and fasting" (Mathew 17: 21)

Be encouraged to fast and pray, for God's call upon your life to manifest.

Exercises to be done:

Drink a laxative to cleanse your system.

Pray and ask God to lead you in this. You are the healed of the LORD; you can do all things through Christ Jesus, who strengthens you.

Do a liquid fast for three days, from 6:00 am to 6:00 pm.

Pray in your Prayer language.

Praise and worship God, in the Beauty of Holiness.

Notes:

Write your experience, before and after. The difficulties you experience. Are your sense of smell and taste heightened? Do you appreciate food more? What are the change in the types of food you want to eat? What about your spiritual senses. Do you find that you are more sensitive to the Holy Ghost more? Let the Holy Spirit guide you as you fast and pray

Bibliography

1. The Holy Bible: Authorized King James Version
USA: Thomas Nelson, 2001

2. Roberts, Frances J., <u>Come away my Beloved:</u> The intimate devotional classic
Ohio: Barbour Publishing, 1970